THE WORLD'S MOST EXTRAORDINARY PEOPLE ...AND ME

MARK DOLAN

THE WORLD'S MOST EXTRAORDINARY PEOPLE ...AND ME

HarperCollins*Publishers*

HarperCollins*Publishers*
77–85 Fulham Palace Road,
Hammersmith, London W6 8JB

www.harpercollins.co.uk

First published by HarperCollins*Publishers* 2010

1 3 5 7 9 10 8 6 4 2

All images provided by Dragonfly Film & Television Productions Limited with the exception of the following images, which were provided by the author: p1 (top), p3 (all), p8 (bottom).

A catalogue record of this book is available from the British Library

ISBN 978-0-00-736487-9

Printed and bound in Great Britain by
Clays Ltd, St Ives plc

This book is dedicated to
anyone who doesn't 'fit in'.

CONTENTS

INTRODUCTION

Over the last three years, I've met some of the world's most extraordinary people. Normally, the term extraordinary is used with more than a generous dose of poetic licence. Not here. The human beings I've encountered are some of the rarest examples of what nature has to offer up, both in the physical and the mental form. People so utterly alien to what is familiar, that they make a hopeful on *Britain's Got Talent* look almost normal. I've been in the company of the tallest woman on earth, the smallest man, the cleverest child (according to their parents at least), the largest families, and the most enhanced women (yes, OK, largest breasts). I've examined at close range the hair on the face of the hairiest man on Earth, and I've even embarked on a road trip with a man so hooked on plastic surgery, he has literally turned himself into a cat.

There was a fierce debate about whether some of these individuals were really record breakers. Some, such as the diminutive men, had their claim for being shortest confirmed in seconds, with the help of my B&Q tape measure. But whatever the measuring technique, which sometimes boiled down to good honest judgement, I gained unprecedented access to a whole range of human beings who are *officially* extraordinary. People whose physical attributes, whether God-given, or courtesy of a dodgy plastic surgeon in Brazil, mark them out as true one-offs, in the strict definition of the term. Phenomena of nature. People born or butchered to be so demonstrably different from the norm that the footprints they make on the human story are indelible.

Alongside the people I met who were born different were those who chose different. Like the appropriately named Mohammed Daad, a sexed-up, one-legged pensioner in the Emirates who, at the time of writing this, had spawned his 84th child. Reassuringly, more than one exhausted woman was involved. This man was the Hugh Hefner of the Middle East, even though, under the unforgiving Arabian sun, his harem looked more bunny boiler than *Playboy* bunny. People like Mr Daad are unique because they have opted for a lifestyle which, for most of us, would at best be described as absurd, and at worst as undiluted hell. And they have made choices which take an iron will, money, tears, blood and a massive amount of human fortitude. But why do they do it? And how do they do it?

Examining motives proved to be a central question in my journeys. Not only the motives of the person at the heart of the story, but more tellingly, those around them. The drunken brother-in-law claiming to be the unique person's agent, the 'loving husband' who struck me as a glorified pimp, the proud parent eager to get his seven year old out of school and into university.

I really wanted to uncover why someone would choose such a wildly different lifestyle from the norm, and why, if you look different because of an incredibly rare genetic or medical condition, you would choose to make a career out of that. All too often I found it was the influence of someone else, whether driven by lust, pride, financial opportunism or just an instinctive desire to be around someone that is, for want of a better word, special. But were these other, shadowy figures well meaning, assisting that person to profit from their rare talent? Or were they no better than the bejewelled 'assistants' who guided Elvis to his last loo break?

It wasn't enough, and it wouldn't be enough, to get to the tallest woman in the world - allegedly Yao Defen in Shanghai, China - say hello, get the tape measure out, and then go home. Or to have my eye nearly taken out by the largest breasts in the world, congratulate their owner and then politely leave. The whole purpose of the endless air miles I notched up (Al Gore hates me) was to know the real person behind the well-distributed photo or YouTube clip. Who

is this person? What are they like? How do they feel being different? Are they extraordinary, or surprisingly normal? And is this human fascination with people born different, or who have made extremely unusual choices, actually indicative of something freaky in us? I was convinced these are people we can learn from and *must* learn from, because their journeys as people, whether self-inflicted or genetic, are completely unique. They haven't just taken the road less travelled in life, they've got down on bended knee and built the road themselves. That's primarily why I embarked on this journey. That, and I love those nuts you get on airplanes.

On revisiting these amazing stories, one of the most difficult parts of the process has been deciding who not to include. I was so moved by those vulnerable and brave individuals living life with terrible obesity, like 88-stone Manuel Uribe and 46-stone Michael Herrera; Michael thankfully later found a solution in the form of dramatic gastric surgery and Manuel can be incredibly proud of himself, having lost 28 stone since his peak, and in the process earning himself a Guinness record for his astonishing weight loss. Then there were the other big families I met, including the charming Postigo family in Spain and the equally engaging Shepherds in England. There was Angela Bismarchi, the human Barbie doll from Brazil, Adora Svitak, the 10-year-old literary genius, and the Malms, two sets of married twins who live under the same roof – a typically dysfunctional set-up on paper which appears to work beautifully in reality.

The exciting thing about all of this is that as I retread these steps into the worlds of the extraordinary, I am going to take you with me. I hope you enjoy. I'm a reasonable travelling companion. My socks are always clean and I tend not to snore. Just one thing though, please eat with your mouth closed when you are sitting next to me, and also, may I politely ask you bring your own supply of chocolate. I share everything, but not chocolate. And finally, before we go any further, you ought perhaps to know just a little bit more about me. I'll spare you the lengthy CV and instead, given its relevance to these journeys, will just briefly speed you back to my seven-year-old self …

I'm an unlikely traveller. I grew up in London and until the age of eighteen I'd mainly been to Tenerife, Ireland and Scotland. Does Scotland count as travelling? Probably only if you walk there. In a gorilla suit, for charity. So all in all, it wasn't the most impressive travel CV. But my *people* CV, on the other hand, is a little bit better. Though I hadn't clocked up many air miles by the time these journeys into the extraordinary had started, I had spent my life genuinely preoccupied with people.

I was born in and grew up above a lively and friendly public house in Camden, North London. In it, I had access to a steady stream of characters, some sober, some not, who

generated an astonishing amount of colour into the early and formative part of my life. As a child, I would come home from school at half past four in the afternoon, satchel round my shoulder and enter my home via the public bar. As I made a beeline for the door (next to the crisps) marked 'private', I would invariably be sucked into a chat with a pensioner or a builder or a taxi driver; take your pick. At that moment I would be entreated to regale them with tales about what I'd learnt from school that day. I remember being roundly, but warmly, lambasted for having English lessons, given that I could clearly already speak the language.

Invariably, however, the great tales being regaled were coming from them. As a child, I suspect I was a somewhat unthreatening figure to whom the most revealing and emotive things could be said. And given this was a public house, the various tipples my father had on sale doubtless helped loosen their tongues and lengthen their memories. Given my parents are from the Republic of Ireland, Sir Robert Peel public house had a slightly Irish skew, though in fact the clientele was a fairly authentic cross-section of the London public.

I was the recipient of endless pieces of advice about the philosophy of life – what's important, what's not, what mistakes not to make and what mistakes *to* make. Pubs are reflective places, where people put their tools down and leave their troubles at the door. It's a haven from all of life's sharpness, even though it may be the very thing responsible for some of life's sharpness too. It's an environment in which to wax lyrical, escape, and, of course, to dream. So to be a bystander to all of this was not only a great privilege but rather addictive. Myself and my brother and my two sisters had access to a whole world downstairs, beneath our home. In fact downstairs was home as well; it was just a bit smokier. And I don't know what it is about pubs, but you seem to get the best 'characters' in them. I'm not sure what defines a 'character'; you will have your own definition. But we can probably agree it's someone who has something about them that is so unique and quirky and a bit dysfunctional, that makes them both engaging and perhaps amusing. There are plenty in showbusiness; it's a haven for oddballs, but it's often hard to judge how genuine their quirkiness it is, and how much of it is a career move. But in any pub in the land, like the one down the road from where you are right now, there will be one or two people in there that are just different. Tragic, funny, insanely clever, weird, rude or, if you're damn lucky, all of the above.

And while I find every person interesting - much to the opprobrium of anyone who happens to be with me when I'm getting on a bus, buying a coffee or just walking down the street - clearly there are those splendid few who have that certain something that turns our heads; something that makes you listen up, and that sometimes makes you want to

run away. On one of my many flights recently, this occurred to me. I am doing now, what I did then, when I was seven years old. I am mooching around the place, looking for interesting people, keeping my mouth shut and letting them tell me their stories. I couldn't tell you now, and I couldn't tell you when I started the journeys, precisely how it's done. I only know that my approach is to keep an open mind and hesitate to judge for as long as possible. And to see the best in people wherever possible. The *World's ... and Me* television series is a souped-up version of those early childhood journeys I made around the saloon bar of Sir Robert Peel pub. Then, as now, meeting a new person was like opening the first page of a new book. You are engaged enough to pick it up, but have no idea how it will play out. This I find immeasurably exciting, and it's what gets me out of bed in the morning. My life became my job for a while, which is cool. Now, with your help, and with the glorious power of hindsight, I'm going to go back there, to revisit these people and these places, and to look again. With fresh eyes, and without the jetlag. I sincerely hope you enjoy the ride. First stop, Vegas ...

THE WORLD'S MOST EXTRAORDINARY PEOPLE ...AND ME

CHAPTER 1

The World's Most Enhanced Woman and Me

PART 1

'The boobs were my brainchild'
Minka's story

I arrived in Las Vegas Nevada, and although a glance at the calendar on my Blackberry would confirm it was 2008, on arrival at the airport, it quickly became apparent that in Vegas it always was, and always will be, 1982.

I'm barely off flight BA766, and having bid farewell to UK civility and proper tea – and having tricked myself through passport control by trying to make the nature of this particular documentary sound as dull as possible so as not to stir the notoriously scabrous US customs officials – I'm greeted by a whole land of slot machines and crap tables. In fact it feels like you've come off the plane and walked straight into Trump Tower. There must be people who have fluttered

away their fortune before even getting their bags off the carousel.

And the airport sets the tone for the whole town – fusty, chintzy and a little bit dog-eared. This airport, like Vegas itself, was genuinely glamorous and gilded and shiny, but a rather long time ago. I'd say it was around the time Peter Duncan was doing his screen test for *Blue Peter*, and when Margaret Thatcher was putting together her first cabinet. The airport carpet tells the whole story. It's an Eighties psychedelic take on the kind of rich pile variety enjoyed by patrons of a typical Wetherspoon pub in the North of England. A heavy, dizzying pattern that feeds into the sense that a visit here will be eye-catching but neither pleasant, nor pretty.

Out of the airport, I experience three seconds of dry, dead Nevada heat hitting my pale, jetlagged skin, before jumping into my hired Toyota SUV, a machine that has been air conditioned to sub-Arctic levels. In fact, they have clearly solved the issue of global warming – and the answer, is for all of us to sell our houses and move into US-built Toyota cars. I've never been colder. My visit to the snowdrifts of Inner Mongolia to meet the smallest man in the world, where temperatures sank to below minus 20, felt like a beach holiday compared with my commute into Sin City. In fact my travels have given me a mild phobia of air conditioning. If you are going out for a night on the tiles in Vegas, or Hong Kong, or Dubai (I'm showing off now), may I suggest you dress for a particularly harsh Edinburgh winter.

Driving into this bizarre experiment of a town is indeed a surreal experience. It goes something like this: airport, then arid desert, then rubbish suburban bit (imagine a very hot Ipswich) and finally a version of Blackpool on a combination of crack cocaine, crystal meth and a particularly strong mug of builders' tea. It's like nothing you've seen in your life. But so is downtown Kabul – that doesn't make it a good thing.

Vegas is a debauched, energy-guzzling, dollar-shredding party that runs 24 hours a day, 365 days a year and has been throbbing in the desert for about the last sixty years. It is the dark heart of the American dream, flying in the face of the USA's predominantly evangelical Christian, puritanical culture. It's like LA in that it's a very wrong place, but like so many wrong things in life (liquorice, crushed denim, Russian pop music) it's strangely comforting to know it's there.

Vegas is all about scale, and inspiring awe. Just in the same way that churches and mosques and synagogues, and whatever it is Quakers hang around in, are designed to make you feel small and create a sense of a higher power, so here in Vegas you feel dwarfed by the size of everything, and the blinding brightness of it all. Driving the Land Cruiser into this adults-only playground, you are struck by a number of familiar sights – a mini version of the Eiffel Tower, a shrunk-down

Venice and of course a pint-sized copy of New York City. The message to Americans outside Vegas is: shred your passport, everything that's good about the world is right here. What a relief to know you'll never have to worry your pretty little head about going to Paris ever again.

The huge problem with Vegas for me is that I'm not a gambler. So it's like being a child in a pub – what's the point? If you don't gamble, you bypass the whole purpose of the place, rendering the experience utterly meaningless (once you've been to the mall, taken in the Bette Midler Show and bought an Abercrombie polo shirt designed for someone ten years younger than you, and considerably more 'ripped'). It's like going to Disneyland but not going on the rides, or going to Florence and keeping your eyes shut.

But then, I wasn't here for the gambling. I'm here to meet the most enhanced woman in the world. But what does that mean? Well, it's a polite euphemism for the female that's had the largest breast implants on Earth. In fact, as I pored over some images of such women on the internet – by way of research you understand – it became quite clear that it was anything but 'enhanced'. Butchered, inflated, almost exploding would be better terms. We all know that boob jobs are now widely practised across the globe. In the UK alone, the best part of 30,000 women a year build on what God has given them, resulting in varying degrees of Dolly Partonness. In the States it's 340,000. That's a lot of breast.

The World's Most Enhanced Woman and Me

Up till now I've been fairly agnostic about the issue of fake boobs. I tend to adopt the crooked nose rule, which is that if you feel the way you look is abnormal, and you just want to fix that, and it will boost your confidence, it's pretty loathsome for someone to say you can't. I'm imagining the equivalent to the crooked nose in the chest region would be a feeling of being so small that there's the absence of a so-called feminine figure. A bit of well-placed silicone might balance things out a bit. In which case, good luck to you.

The women I've come to see are not the thick end of the wedge. They are off the wedge. They are on another planet. They are their own species. They occupy a chapter of their own in the big book of human madness. Minka is one such woman. And of course, she lives in Vegas. Elsewhere, with her matching 4-litre-enhanced breasts, she might be an embarrassment, or worse, a freak. Here in the neon-lit desert, she's a national treasure – she's Vegas's answer to Rolf Harris. She, along with a few other ageing, living 'legends', plies a trade here as a porn star, glamour model and semi-professional tennis player. From a glance online, it's very much in that order. And it's time to meet her.

I'm staying in one of the Pyramids – the gold-leaf Egyptian paradise that is the Luxor Hotel. It's a Pyramid on the outside, but rather more Travelodge once you get to your room. After having breakfast at one of the hotel's 870 branches of Starbucks, I fired up my trusty mini space rocket on wheels and

drove to Minka's home – an upmarket residential district a mile or two from the Strip. Minka clearly likes to be near the shop. It's a glorious, dry, sunny day. But that's not a story here. And my attempts at weather small talk in this town are met with death stares. Granted, good weather-related small talk relies on the weather having some kind of narrative. Stuff has to happen. The weather here is like listening to a Westlife album, it's more, and more, and more, of the same.

I'm always a bit nervous about meeting people for the first time, particularly if they are the first contributor in a new film. Meeting the people who I've spent weeks or months trying to get hold of, and deliberating as to whether in the world they occupy they are the right choice, that's the scary bit. So as I walk up Minka's driveway, past her gleaming white Mercedes-Benz E Class, paid for no doubt by her army of online fans, I'm tense. There's a lot riding on that first moment. We have to hit it off. I'm going to spend a number of days with this person. They have to like me. They have to open up the outer and inner workings of their life to a 6 ft 5 in, bespectacled Limey they've never met before. Try as I might to make a good impression, it's all futile – it's not in my hands. The door knocker is, and I whack it. Then I ring the doorbell. Then I hammer the wood of the door with my knuckle. I always like to take advantage of the myriad solutions by which those inside a house are alerted to the presence of someone on the outside. In the same way I will select

the up and down buttons while waiting for a lift, even though I'm only going up. I like the idea the lifts are working for me.

Dogs, many of them, have heard my hammering. They are yapping away. The person the other side of the door chides them and unlocks a seemingly endless series of locks. The door opens fractionally, just enough for what looks like a squirrel in a wig to bomb it through the gap, into the front yard and onto the road. I chase across the road, dodging a postal truck, and aim to get this little canine runt back to its owner. We can't start this encounter with the death of a beloved pooch - not on my watch. Dog in hand, I hurry back along the driveway and through Minka's ornate, faux-antique front porch. Minka closes the door behind me. There are dogs everywhere. They are all small, loud and identical. At least six, but who knows ... There might have been twenty. It was in a blur of dog. But, not being indelicate, this is the perfect way to meet a woman as notoriously chesty as Minka. Because as she bent over, and tried in vain to gather her screeching flock, her breasts perambulated like two lead-filled beachballs, glued to a tanned broomstick. There is no photograph which does adequate justice to the sheer scale of Minka's swinging décolletage. And where do you look? Hitherto I have summoned up every ounce of my Irish Roman Catholic guilt to avert my gaze at the sight of a woman's cleavage. But now it's impossible. This is the breasts equivalent of a twelve-car pile-up on the M1. You're not going to not look. Minka's hunched position and a hopelessly low-cut lycra sports tube conspire to produce a sight which makes the collapse of the Berlin Wall look a tad uneventful. Eventually she stands up. That in itself is a sight to behold.

The dogs safely locked behind a child safety gate, it's time to properly greet Minka.

'Hello Minka! Great to meet you!' Minka seems nonplussed at what I thought was an uncontroversial opening remark. There's an awkward pause. She then helloes me back. But that's all I get. This is playing out like an audience with the Queen. Minka is very tanned, and surprisingly slim. In fact she's tiny. Her delicate East Asian frame, complete with a waist like a serviette ring, plays host to what may be the largest enhanced breasts on God's Earth. But does Minka want to meet me? Does she want me to be there at all? The opening vibes suggest not. This is very troubling. Minka is passive, almost not with it, and seems to have tuned out of this encounter before it's even started. Luckily there was someone who clearly did want me there. And as I turned around in the hallway of this rather tall house, he was walking down the grand, curved staircase. In his slippers. It was time to meet Hank ...

To add to the surrealism of Minka's utterly incongruous body was the arrival of a man who would introduce himself as Minka's 'manager'. Curiously, unnervingly, he bore an uncanny resemblance to the Hollywood screen idol

Humphrey Bogart. Everything, down to the dark, slick-back hair, the full eyebrows, the massive man's head on a tiny man's body, and the general air of lugubriousness. Also like Bogie, Woody has a set of shoulders that seem to be in an almost permanent state of shrug. And both men even share the same watery, tragic eyes. Though the tears come from different places.

I rush to the bottom of the staircase.

'Hi, I'm Mark,' I say enthusiastically.

He extends his hand. 'I'm Hank,' he says dryly.

'Hi Hank.'

'I mean Woody,' he says.

This is a confusing start. I've fallen at the first hurdle. His name.

'So Woody is your real name?'

With a hint of aggression he counters: 'No no no. I just gave you my real name.' He then laughs nervously, like a mafia boss waiting for the guns to arrive. 'My stage name is Woody.'

God, this is confusing. So what does he do?

'I'm Minka's manager,' he says. At this point Minka, a vision in lycra, is standing, hands on hips, seeming to enjoy the early focus on her little helper, rather than herself.

'And this lady is a full-time occupation – right?' I'm scrambling for the right thing to say, so that this encounter doesn't fall apart around my ears. At this point Woody – or Hank, or whatever he's called – is tense, like a cat being held upside down in the air. I'm on his territory and I'm far from reassuring him that this will all be OK for him.

'More or less she is, yeah,' he concedes.

'So this lady here is big business, right?'

A quick glance at those personal twin towers of hers, jammed into her lycra boob tube, which seemed anything but ladylike.

'She's a commodity,' Woody continues, warming to his theme. 'There's only one like her in the world.'

It's like he's describing the Statue of Liberty. But did large numbers of people jump on a ferry and pay to go inside Minka? We'll get to that later ...

Woody is now firmly settling into his manager's role. He continues to explain her unique selling point(s). 'There's only one like her in the world. Have you ever seen an Asian that looks like that?'

'No, I don't suppose I have,' I say, embarrassed that we are talking about this woman like she is a rare Pekingese.

Woody seems to assume we are all unofficial shareholders in Minka Inc. He's talking to me in cold, factual terms about this human being that's looking on, which I find very awkward. I have the early sense that it's because Woody lives in Woody's world, a world he thinks we all live in. There's no sense that this tall, bespectacled Limey standing in his house – and I think it's his house (he seems to be wearing pyjamas)

– might think it's somewhat strange to refer to someone, anyone, as a 'commodity'. And this particular commodity was, I suspected, more than just his client.

We wander into the living room. Like the rest of the house, it has its own colour spectrum which ranges from off white, to very off white. It's that classic Martha Stewart inspired look of suburban American grandeur. Faux-mahogany kitchen units, fibreglass counter posing as marble, carpet heavier and thicker than Brian Blessed's beard, massive, deep, low easy chairs and a telly the size of a football pitch. It's the American dream. And it's identical to every other similarly moneyed house in the country. Curiously, it's not just in the malls that America rolls out its monolithic, chain-store culture. It's often been proudly boasted that if you eat a hamburger from McDonalds, it will taste the same in Kentucky as it does in San Francisco. Similarly, a middle-class living room in Connecticut will be a dead ringer for one in Kansas City. I can prove that this is true, in an entirely unscientific manner, but born out of experience. I've stood in around twenty living rooms in America, and apart from the pecuniary value of the various items therein, and the layout of the respective houses, they were all essentially the same inside. Even my beloved Auntie Pasty's house in Napa is decorated in the same way as Minka's. Which is confusing. Maybe I'm just guilty of the interior decor equivalent of casual racism – because these homes are foreign to me,

they all 'look the same'. I hasten to add that notwithstanding decor parallels, that's where Auntie Patsy's and Minka's similarities abruptly end.

Minka rushes off to an ice cooler and offers me a crisp, chilled apple. In spite of these undoubtedly unhealthy protrusions she calls breasts, she does have a strangely healthy glow. She clearly maintains her body to almost Madonnaesque standards. She is tanned and toned. And frankly just the act of standing up from a chair, given her upper proportions, is a gym exercise all of its own. We get onto her record, and whether she holds one.

'So Minka ...' I start. How do I put this? 'Do you have the most enhanced breasts in the world?' That's how you put this.

'No' she replies, flatly. Her voice is deep and her English, both in terms of pronunciation and grammar, is regularly upstaged by her mother tongue of Korean.

'You don't have the most enhanced breasts in the world. OK, where would you say you come in the order of it?' I ask.

'Number two.'

'Who's number one?'

'Maxi. But I don't know what happened – she got infection. But I don't know what happened. Her boob, one is gone – I cannot find out what happened. When she's gone, I'm gonna be number one.'

Woody is shaking his head disconsolately. 'We don't know that for sure,' he mutters. Minka, the Pekingese, is off

the leash, and he doesn't like it. I don't know why Woody is suddenly so circumspect about the facts. I suspect he's a player in this world of large-breasted females, and therefore not one to spit on his own d-cup. Claims about who's biggest in this arena would doubtless lead to a nasty catfight among these top-heavy women. A call later to Maxi's agent informs me that Maxi does indeed seem to be out of the picture at the moment, whether retired or otherwise – and is thus out of this rather perverse race.

'So Minka,' I go on, 'if Maxi's out of action, does that mean you have the largest enhanced breasts in the world?'

'Yes,' she says without fanfare.

'You're number one!' I insist.

'Yes!' And now, for the first time, Minka seems to be perking up – her pink lip gloss emulsioning a sincere smile. She's warming to the attention and focus. Unexpectedly she dances towards me and grabs my arm.

'Give me your hand,' she says playfully.

At this moment I'm seized by a paralysis called Englishness. She pulls my hand with her veiny, gym-fit arm, her South Korean biceps gently pulsing. She then pushes my hand under the vast cantilever that is her right bosom. It's like being asked to have a quick hold of the flat roof at Heathrow Terminal 5. Her breasts are incalculably heavy – the figure of 4000 centilitres of volume per breast doesn't do it justice. And what's shocking isn't just the dense weight. Or

how it looks. It's the tactile aspect. The breast is rock hard, like a block of concrete. The kind of concrete they use to hold bridges up. In windy countries. That get earthquakes.

It's at this point that any sense of camp, seaside-postcard comedy disappears out of the room. The price Minka pays in every waking and sleeping hour has suddenly dawned on me. Having been initially perturbed and certainly repulsed by Minka's inflated upper half, it now strikes me as being horrific, like someone living with a terrible disability. Except this is self-inflicted. Or Woody-inflicted ...

'Are they heavy – you think that's heavy?' says Minka.

Why's she asking this insanely silly question? Yes! Does she need confirmation that carrying a rack equivalent to *six* large Evian bottles strapped to your front is rather laboursome? I suspect it's her way of garnering some understanding on the part of others about just what she's going through, and that she can carry this much weight and not be dead by now. I also take it as a sign that Minka is starting to trust me, and that perhaps she feels increasingly comfortable with my approach and my motivation for being there.

As my sympathy for this remarkable woman grows, so does my germinating affection. In spite of her astonishing appearance, she is strikingly normal. And I detect a strength, not just in her lower back.

'That weighs a ton – how do you carry that around all the time?' I ask.

Woody pipes up, Alistair Campbell-mode, rapid rebuttal.

'She works out every day.'

Oh, well that's OK then ...

Having literally come to grips with Minka's body, it's clear to me that these huge breasts can only stay put for a finite period of time. But how long precisely?

Woody's in no doubt: 'Ten years.'

Minka, like a teenager indulging in backchat, says sulkily, 'He says ten years.'

I innocently suggest to Woody that's a long time to carry that kind of weight around.

Minka doesn't give Woody a chance to respond.

'That's right – you are right ...' she says, glaring at Woody. I now feel I'm in the middle of a fight these two are pretending not to have. It's awkward. Wading into choppier waters I ask Minka the question again, the one Woody has answered for her.

'What about you, Minka, what's your timescale?'

'I don't know, maybe two or three more years,' she suggests.

Woody's state of permanent shrug has notched up to a passive rage.

I feed the monster.

'Woody, if she said to you I'm going to see the plastic surgeon tomorrow, I'm going to have it all out because I want to have a normal life, what happens?'

'I'm out of here ...' he says dismissively.

'What do you mean by that?'

'I'm out of here. What would you say? Businesswise – businesswise – it's gone.'

Minka, still in fifteen-year-old mode, says 'fine'. Like it's not fine.

Woody continues the lecture. 'Because she knows she's gotta keep 'em till she's got enough money to retire, so long as she's not fat she can remain till maybe she's seventy years old ...'

What??

He goes on, back to his favourite part of the sales pitch. 'She's a commodity. Coz there's no one in the world like her. No one – that's it.'

So several things have emerged in this subtly explosive chat. First of all, Woody is more than Minka's 'manager'. They reside together, and in fact I am to discover later that they are married and even have a son. Woody is defensive about protecting Minka's image to her fans as sexy, single and available. I have to respect this. Minka might be at the glamour, or even, sleazy end of the entertainment industry, but anyone in a magazine, TV show or movie has to perpetuate a certain persona that plays to their fanbase's fantasy. It's the nature of showbusiness. That's why for all those years, we had to labour under the illusion George Michael was straight. And that Little and Large were funny.

But what's disturbing is that Minka and Woody do not have a united front, on Minka's front. This is genuinely troubling. It doesn't seem that Minka is the driving force in this quest for mammoth breastage. I am concerned that Woody's perception of his wife as a commodity supersedes any husbandly concerns for her physical well-being or, at the very least, her physical comfort. Otherwise why would he bark that she can carry those edifices around until she's seventy, when she clearly wants to have them out in a year or two? Surely it's her call, isn't it? A man of Woody's generation might not have included Germaine Greer or Naomi Wolf in his bedtime reading (I had Woody down as a strictly Wilbur Smith man; no offence Wilbur...), but surely the most misogynistic, unreconstructed male wouldn't question a woman's sovereignty over her body and what goes into it? Would he?

The problem comes back to Minka being both a commodity and a wife. The ultimate conflict of interest. With her long mane of oriental hair and proud posture, Minka isn't unlike a prize racehorse and Woody her diminutive jockey, complete with whip. I can see how their marriage, and the life they live, is based on Minka's breasts. This woman is an emotional and economic prisoner in her own body. How terrifying is that? Imagine being owned by your own body. Now obviously the likes of Kate Moss have to eat a lot of salad to keep the body they are selling, and an athlete certainly doesn't always feel like getting up at 5 a.m. to go running, to stay at the top of his or her game. But Minka's sacrifice is one which affects totally, let there be no doubt about this, her quality of life. And almost unquestionably her health.

One clue to this is that getting to be as big as Minka is now illegal in the United States, and the technology with which she inflated her chest is no longer available. Minka is one of a handful of 'living legends' in the world of big breasts and Woody is right to suggest that there's no one like her anywhere else on Earth. That's because Minka is part of the rarefied 'silly string' generation. A tiny group of women who experimented in the early 1990s with a special material which produces fantastically enormous breasts. It's impossible to be as big as Minka with silicone, as silicone is an extremely dense, heavy material. Gravity would prevail. So various plastic surgeons experimented with a material developed during the Vietnam war to help heal open wounds. This special fabric fuses with skin tissue and expands with water and matter to form an extra skin, for where it had been blown off by an understandably belligerent Vietnamese soldier. This doctor speculated that something which does this for a wound may have the same effect in the cosmetic arena. The results were startling. Women like Minka had the silly string inserted and day by day their breasts grew in size. To the point where it was feared the breasts might eventually explode. Indeed some of the early recipients of this procedure went back to have their breasts drained as they were getting so big.

Mercifully this practice was later outlawed amid concern about the health risks. But a tiny number of now ageing 'silly string' ladies - Minka, Maxi Mounds and Caila Cleavage - still trade on their look because essentially it's impossible to look like that now. So they have a unique selling point, albeit a freakish one. They are the embodiment of a frankly disturbing period in the history of plastic surgery. They reflect a time when plastic surgeons were about as vigorously regulated as your local hairdresser, and when the patients were human guinea pigs, willing participants in an extremely risky experiment that might ultimately claim their lives. And they paid for the privilege. One such victim was Lolo Ferrari. Lolo's story is a well-known one, and her untimely, mysterious death casts a dark hue over this world of big breasts. And perhaps that is her legacy. Because not only is it almost impossible to be that big in the twenty-first century, but with Lolo's passing, the comedy of her appearance - often paraded on TV shows like *Eurotrash* - segued, almost instantly, into the macabre, and tragic.

Woody and Minka met in Minka's native South Korea when Woody was in the military. Given the age gap between them, and the fact that Woody brought her to the USA, a picture was emerging of a relationship, both in business terms and personally, that was unequal. Apart from the money, I want to get a sense of what motivated Woody in this whole endeavour. Is Minka's appearance purely business?

'Woody, do you think that Minka's look is attractive?' I ask.

'I ... yes. I like big-breasted women, personally always have,' he says.

'So you're a big boob man,' I say.

'Yeah,' he says.

'As far as you're concerned, you've lucked out then,' I suggest.

'Yeah,' he says. Then there's a crunching gear change I don't see coming. 'If it wasn't for her I'd be dead – that's one thing.'

Eh? I'm not expecting this. What does he mean?

'I have cancer,' he says.

'Do you?'

'Yeah – I've been in remission for nine years,' he says, rightly proudly.

I shake his hand by way of approbation. And view him as a human being for the first time in our encounter. Over on the small dinner table, one of the Chihuahuas is licking from the bowl of someone's unfinished breakfast.

'Yes, I'm a cancer survivor,' he says.

'Congratulations,' I say. 'So why do you feel she's helped you survive cancer?'

'Coz she's taken care of me.'

'Right,' I say. We've got pathos here. It's emotional. Woody's eyes are filling with even more water than before. The juxtaposition of this pornographer being cared for by

his wank-fantasy nurse/wife takes the bizarre nature of this union to a new level. It's like Iris Murdoch and John Bayley, but with massive tits. I'm already looking forward to the film, starring Jim Broadbent as Woody.

'Whereas probably no one in my condition one year ago would have took care of me like that ...'

Minka's full lips turn upwards. Oh my God, she loves him. I'm confused. And so I should be. That's love.

We go upstairs on the softest, mushiest carpet I've ever stepped on. The Americans do mushy like no one else. The carpets are mushy, the suspension on their cars is mushy and 98 per cent of the food is too. Americans like things to be soft and squashy. I think it fits in with the first of the two American obsessions: comfort and convenience.

We make our way conveniently up the staircase to 'the office', inside which is a large computer, an ironing board and a green parrot. The parrot is called Buddy and he is Woody's. Why do certain members of families appropriate certain animals? Surely if an animal lives under one roof, it belongs to all the inhabitants. Rusty was our gorgeous German Shepherd when I was growing up. He belonged to me, my brother, my two sisters, and my parents. In fact he belonged to hundreds of people, as I grew up above a pub in Camden in London, and anyone who purchased a pint of Ruddles County, or Carlsberg, essentially bought a share of Rusty as he meandered around the pub hoovering up

discarded Golden Wonder Prawn Cocktail crisps. But he was no fat pet. More on them later ...

To prove his ownership of the soul of this parrot, Woody essentially proceeds to French kiss the creature. This is a difficult thing to watch. Which is saying something in a room which contains over a thousand hard-core pornographic DVDs. None of which, mercifully, feature Buddy. Minka does though. We look at one DVD cover – it's Minka with naked breast exposed, being licked by another, fair-haired lady.

'Is that a friend?' I ask. 'Who is that lady?'

'That's Maxi Mounds,' says Woody. This is the legendary Maxi Mounds, the most enhanced woman in the world, on paper at least. But as a quick call to her agent confirmed, she is currently retired. It's hard to picture a woman that looks like that being 'retired'. I can't picture her playing for pennies at a local bridge club, or wandering the aisles of B&Q, looking for solar-powered garden lamps. Maybe she just knits.

'Woody, I've just noticed one of the films there is *The Milking of Minka*,' I say. I suspect it's thin on plot. 'And then there is another one called *The Orient Express*, what's the storyline in that one?'

'It's the Orient *Sexpress*,' corrects Woody.

I wasn't playing dumb. That's how green I am about these things – I actually missed the very demonstrative pun. I go on reading the blurb about it. 'Starring Minka, Mr Hanks ... Is that Tom Hanks?' Now I am playing dumb.

'That was me,' says Woody.

'Oh, you were in one of those movies?'

'I have done a lot of the movies with her.'

This is a surprise – I didn't have Woody down as front of house. So it turns out, like Bogart, his doppelganger, he has a career on celluloid too. Though I suspect *The Orient Sexpress* isn't quite the cinematic masterpiece that *Casablanca* is.

'So you have starred in these adult movies, most of the movies?' I ask.

'Yes, because there is things she will do with me in a video that she won't do with other guys.'

'OK,' I say.

He goes on. 'She will do me orally without a condom, but she hasn't done that lately and she has got to go back, she has got to go back to doing the nasty stuff for it to sell.'

I go on to ask him what the nasty stuff is. He gives me an example.

'Well, do you know the expression cream pie?' he asks.

'No I don't.' I don't.

'It's when a guy comes into the woman and you have a close-up of the vagina as the semen comes out,' he says nonchalantly.

The expression 'I wish I hadn't asked' can't be more appropriate at this juncture. And I have had those moments in the past. I've asked plenty of women who were overweight when the baby was due. And, enquiring as to how long they were staying with us, I asked a gravely ill friend, 'When do we lose you?' Thankfully they actually survived, and spared my blushes ...

But asking Woody to elaborate on the context of the 'nasty stuff' is my gravest error. Aside from the misfortune of being presented with this image in my mind, I am amazed at Woody's sheer boredom at describing these things. It's like when the heroes of the trenches during the First World War became very sanguine, nay flippant, about death and images of death, so Woody is a veteran of the sex industry and thus has a certain attitude to the human body and its reproductive processes, which is reflected in the language he uses. But how can you possibly talk about your wife in these terms? It struck me at the time as cold and brutal, and even now, looking back on it, fills me with a sadness.

But the flipside of it is they are married and she did nurse him through cancer and I think they genuinely care for each other. Love comes in all shapes and sizes and though I felt sorry for one of the parties involved, ultimately their relationship functions. It works and each partner has a set of duties and expectations on them which are wholly unconventional and unedifying, but that is the relationship. It's ironic to think that this dysfunctional union has escaped the statistic of one in three marriages failing. Woody and Minka, for all of the horror of their domestic arrangements, are still together after all these years. And they clearly need each other.

'Minka, how do you feel about this, this business of having to do the nasty stuff?' I ask. She is leaning on the ironing board, which is creaking at the combined weight of her, and her breasts.

'Hmm, I have to do it, I have to do it. They want to see something different, you know. I have to do it. It's money yeah. Income,' she says.

I feel that she's rehearsing the party line. But she believes it too. That said, there is no enthusiasm in her answer. It strikes me as a doleful acceptance of the status quo. They do live in a big house. They have cars, jewellery, and huge medical bills (welcome to America). Minka has certain material expectations which trap her in a job she would rather not be doing. But while plenty of people compromise professionally to keep themselves in iPods, foreign holidays and posh sausages, few have to make their bodies available to the latest well-hung movie star. And even fewer have to pay the 24/7 price of carrying these monsters around, even when asleep. Minka's never off duty from her own body.

'But is money really worth it for what, you know, for what you go through?' I ask Minka, pushing this point.

'Money, money, power. Money control whole, all over the world. Right?' she says.

Woody fires up, almost evangelically. 'You can't live without money,' he announces. 'The bottom line, this is a

business; any business the bottom line is money and you got to do what you got to do to make the money.'

Minka then interjects, supporting Woody. They've cornered me. It's good cop, bad cop. Big-boobed cop.

'They want to see something different, you know. I have to do it. It's money yeah. Income,' she says.

She seems convinced. And it's time to experience one of the fruits of Minka's labours now. It's time for Minka's tennis game at her local club. We are on our way in the car. A white Mercedes with cream leather seats. The seats are firm, not mushy. The Germans don't do mushy. Woody has the hang-dog expression of a professional chauffeur as he ferries his VIP with the USPs to her next engagement.

There is a brief, amusing argument about how Minka is flaky when it comes to her financial paperwork. Woody is still sore from a lost three-week period in which Minka didn't put her petrol receipts through the books. Something you'd think would be hard to get cross about, but Woody's rage grows as he recalls this fiscal misdemeanour. There's a serious hue to this discussion though, as at the heart of it Woody is anxious that she couldn't manage on her own without him. A scenario less abstract for him than most, since his brush with the big C. Minka reverts to her inner pouting teenager during this discussion. The look on her face says 'woteva'. She claims none of this is true, though notably she offers no evidence in her defence. I tend to side with Woody on this one. He's clearly business-minded to the core and, like all American citizens, has an acute, vitriolic hatred of paying tax. They continue to and fro with this argument, which has a rehearsed familiarity to it - it feels like one of their argumentative 'greatest hits'. Like a well-meaning child sitting in the back, I change the subject to try to stop 'mummy and daddy' bickering. In much the way I used to try to stop my parents having their occasional ruck. Except I'm not related to these people, and I'm a thirty-five-year-old man.

'So how often do you play tennis?' Trying to sound cheery, to break the tension.

'Every morning,' says Woody grumpily. 'Her world revolves around tennis.'

'Oh really?'

'Her entire lifestyle revolves around tennis,' he repeats.

'Minka ...?'

She doesn't have time to speak.

Woody continues his moan. 'It's interfered with our business.'

'Has it really?'

'Definitely.'

'Sometimes tennis comes first,' I suggest.

'Yeah yeah, and that's when we get to really going at it,' he says.

'That's when you get really fighting?'

'Yeah, I get very, very argumentative when the tennis comes, when she puts the tennis before the business.'

'Do you think the tennis is an escape from the breast business?'

'Yeah yeah it's an escape for her,' he concedes.

He says this with a reluctance, rather than any sense of being pleased for her. Like an uncaring farmer allowing his livestock fresh straw not because that would be nice for them but because they'll die if they don't get it. And that would be inconvenient. We get out of the climate-controlled Benz and step into the climate-uncontrolled Vegas heat. It's lunchtime, the point of the day at which the Nevada sun is at its most unforgiving. The tarmac on the road looks as hot as the day it was laid. Minka is resplendent in an all-white tennis outfit, with that shade of white only a very bleachy washing powder can manage – the kind a generation of babies in the Seventies were subjected to, creating a mini eczema epidemic at that time – ah happy days. In fact her outfit is so bright, pressed and consistently white, she could have been the darling of the Lawn Tennis Association. Though her chest would have the older members of the club spluttering into their English Breakfast tea.

She has invited me for a game. Now at this point, I am reminded that there are almost no things I am good enough at to compete in an actual game. When 'playing tennis', something I have probably done about eight times in my life,

I normally request to my colleague that we play 'Dolan rules', which involves hitting the ball to each other very slowly, the aim being to keep the ball in play. Any obeying of the boundaries of the court would be against Dolan rules. So there's no 'in' or 'out'. The ball is literally inside the court or over the fence, and not in the court. Those are the rules. Serving is a no-no too. Especially with Minka - I would need to be in the car park to return one of her serves. It turns out, in my unqualified opinion, she's extraordinarily good at tennis. She's fast, powerful and accurate. She ignores my gentlemen's agreement about the rules, and plays proper tennis at me. I say 'fucking hell' a lot.

But as with all matters Minka, it always comes back to the breasts - they are the two elephants in the room, as it were. And out there on court, the last thing you will notice is her backhand or volleying. Her untamed bosoms dart around the court quicker that she does. It's actually painful to watch. It looks totally uncomfortable. It's ironic that the one pastime about which she is truly passionate is the one which graphically illustrates the price she has paid - and pays - for her day job. If it wasn't sad it would be amusing. But after having spent time with Minka, having eaten her chilled, crunchy apples, having played with her dogs and having asked her how much she paid for her fridge, I've grown very fond of her. She has a dry sense of humour - often asking me in hushed tones, 'You like blow jobs, Mark?' not because she's being lewd, but she has discovered that kind of chatter makes me uncomfortable. She is intelligent, knowing, wise and funny. But at an earlier age, she met a man from another, more economically robust continent, with big ideas about their future together. A man with a big-breasts fascination, with connections in the pornographic world. So this woman morphed into his wet dream, both in the bedroom, and on the balance sheet. It's now what they both do – and it's hard to change that, especially when one of the parties is doggedly committed to that path, and when the other has a body which says there's no turning back.

I had one last go at cornering Woody as to his role in this path Minka has taken.

'I think the problem is, Woody, that people will think you particularly like big breasts. You have met this young woman in South Korea, you took her to America and they will see that you are very much the driving force in all these really big choices. What do you think of that?' I ask.

'She hasn't done anything that she didn't choose to do, OK?' he counters.

'But is she and also this lifestyle an embodiment of your personal fantasy?'

'No.'

'Even though you like the big boobies?'

'She had big boobs before, they are just bigger now that's all.'

'Quite a bit bigger,' I say, and it's an understatement.

'Which is fine. But she was plenty big before.'

Hmm. I'm not convinced.

This is as far as I feel I'm going to get with Woody. The best I can say about him is that he isn't breaking any laws. But I do feel their relationship is unequal, and unbalanced, like Minka's very body. I just hope at some point she does retire, because although material comfort is alluring to almost all of us, I feel that for Minka it's reached the point at which the material stuff is the tail that wags the dog of their life. Before I leave to pack my bags in my tiny room in one of the Pyramids, I put this to her. Wouldn't she give up the endless strain on her upper body and having to sit by the pool, naked, in her fifties, sixties and even seventies, being photographed for her website by her husband who's telling her, 'Close up. Smile. OK. Turn your butt around ...' Wouldn't she rather be playing tennis?

'When I am playing tennis I am not in the business. Sometime I wanna get out from, you know, I am telling you true, do I love it tennis? I love it. Just bottom line is money.' She says, wiping a bead or two of sweat from her brow.

'But wouldn't you rather live in a small house and drive an old car and then only play tennis?'

'No, no,' she says.

I have my answer, but it's not the one, for her sake, I really want to hear.

Taking one last glance at Minka's iconic décolletage, my eyes are once again assaulted by the stretched, veiny horror of Minka's chest. Brutal, barbaric, inhuman; none of these words overstates the case. The idea that anyone would consider going even a millimetre bigger than this is unthinkable. But these journeys are all about the unthinkable. Meet Sheyla, a young Brazilian television celebrity, who's about to have an operation that will give her an extra litre and a half of size per breast *on top* of what Minka has. That's five and a half litres per breast. And she's almost as petite as Minka. What's she thinking? Can I stop her? The flight's booked; I'm on my way ...

PART 2

The World's Most Enhanced Woman
Sheyla Hershey's story

Well, if Minka is a living legend, and a symbol of a bygone era in terms of enhanced women, Brazilian model and media personality Sheyla Hershey is distinctly about the twenty-first century. Just twenty-three, she boasts a reality show in the US and can even more proudly boast she hasn't so much as taken her top off. Not that the images I see online leave much to the imagination. Pouting glumly at the camera, she looks like a bleach-blonde equivalent of

Posh Spice, but one whose figure suggests she's enjoyed rather a few more steak dinners than Posh has. She is perhaps aping the Marilyn Monroe shape, but with two distinct additions that would have Norma Jean turning in her Hollywood grave. Sheyla lives in Houston, Texas from where she earns an apparently decent living modelling and making numerous TV appearances, including her own reality strand on CBS television. There are lots of references to her online as the Brazilian Jordan – God what a thought.

So why am I swelling my carbon footprint further, to meet this woman? She is, at this moment, flying to Brazil to have another breast augmentation. This, if it goes the way she wants it to go, will increase her breast size to 55 cubic centilitres per breast, which would be a world record. It's too good an opportunity, in exploring this world of enhanced women and what motivates them, to meet a woman who is in the process of getting bigger, or indeed about to be the biggest. Who knows, I might even be able to talk her out of it ...

Sheyla's flying back to Brazil, to a beach town called Villa Bella on the north-east coast of Brazil, where her sister lives. I fly from Vegas to Houston and we then meet up and fly together to Brazil. I was quite anxious about whether she would actually catch the flight, as up until now, on the phone and on email, she's been mercurial to say the least. But something told me, particularly after looking at her website (which is a masterclass in self-promotion), that this was another media appearance she wasn't going to miss.

I wander around Houston Airport, dazed by a heady mix of jetlag and weak American lager. And there she is, standing outside a Hudson News, looking lost. And glamorous. She's wearing what looks like a woollen bra, in tartan, and a matching miniskirt approximately one centimetre in length. All the clothes look incredibly tiny. In keeping with the Mrs Beckham theme, it looks like she has stolen one of Posh's outfits and forgotten she is a size 12, not a size 6. Her skin is caked in a glutinous light-brown make-up/fake tan. She looks like her entire body has been dipped in a vat of the caramel bit of a Cadbury's Caramel. Her hair is blonde and brittle; I'd suggest it's been so long since it was the colour God intended that now even God can't remember what colour it was supposed to be. She's wearing heels that approximate in height to all the Harry Potter books piled on top of each other, and her ability to stand for more than five seconds in them involves a similarly impressive amount of wizardry. And her breasts...

Ah yes. Her breasts. Why we're here. Well, they are very large. But they are not on the Minka scale. Instead she looks like a sexually frustrated cartoonist's impression of a woman. Like a supersized Jessica Rabbit crossed with a Russ Meyer actress, and a bit of Babs Windsor thrown in for good measure. And there is something comical looking about this lady and it's not just her top-heavy profile. She looks more like a character than a real person. She is a sort of walking human caricature. And I'm about to get on an airplane with her. Fortunately we are allocated seats at separate ends of the plane, allowing me to keep my powder dry in terms of questions and avoiding a syndrome the great Les Dawson used to refer to as 'having the fight before you get in the ring'. I sip my Caffeine Free Diet Coke, thus experiencing no physical emotion whatsoever and wait for the hours to pass, only to be occasionally stirred by the sight of the inflated, tartan-clad blonde making her way to the loo. In the context of this flight, she is a vision, an airbrushed, bouncing bombshell, clashing wildly with the grey plastic backdrop of this American Airlines 737 and its jaded passengers.

We arrive in Brazil, and she seems to perk up once she strides into the airport. Every footstep of her faux Jimmy Choos can be heard for miles. The shrill clatter of her heels announces that Sheyla's coming home. She is speaking at double speed, perspiring slightly, and is fidgety. It feels like she is morphing into her public persona and is somehow preparing to put on a show. As we walk through the sliding doors into the public part of the airport, there is the sound of shrieking and general excitement. They are calling out her name. Flashguns on cameras are splashing light onto both of us, and I'm feeling like a spare part, knowing they're not

here for me, but I'm there anyway – a feeling Denis Thatcher undoubtedly had for about three decades. There are perhaps thirty people gathered, with all permutations of camera equipment with which to capture the moment. Bizarrely, in the mêlée, a woman rushes up to me and gives me a hug! Now this is my first time in Brazil, so perhaps this is what happens. Or maybe she has never seen someone quite so tall, thin and pale in her country before, and feels the need to touch me to see if I'm real. With a little help from Sheyla as interpreter, it transpires that *Balls of Steel* – a late-night TV comedy show I presented for Channel 4, is shown in Brazil. This is a surreal interruption to an otherwise surreal arrival. Luckily *Balls of Steel* appears not to be a ratings monster here, as, apart from some odd looks and whispering in an elevator later that day, that's the last time my global fame is to interrupt this journey.

There are placards with Sheyla's name scrawled across them, being held aloft. Quite poorly scrawled. It always amazes me that people who make placards, in all walks of life, couldn't have a better sense of production value. Be it striking workers, protesting students or celebrating football fans, I'm always wondering whatever happened to good quality marker pens, and fabric suited to the painting materials being deployed. And couldn't someone decide in advance what the size and style of the font will be? And surely only the person in the group with the greatest artistic skill and command of the English language should be allowed anywhere near the paint itself. I don't think this is unreasonable.

And speaking of paint, these placards for Sheyla lack the whiff of authenticity. And as there are lingering, emotional hugs all round with her 'fans', it starts to look more like a reunion of family and friends, than the arrival home of a Jordan-like icon. Even the most rabidly ambitious starlet doesn't kiss fans on eight different parts of their face. Interrupting the adulation for a second, I ask, 'So Sheyla, how do they know that you are here?'

'Ah well, like, obviously, I talk with the local news about what's going to—'

'You give them a little tip off?'

'Yeah', she says.

Oh, well that answers that. I'm used, in these journeys, to dealing with people who are as evasive as they are unique. Not Sheyla. It seems it's not just her tights that are transparent. We leave the media scrum (5 per cent local media, 95 per cent uncles and aunties), we jump into a waiting taxi and head to her sister's place, where I've been promised a Brazilian barbeque, which sounds like a violent variation on the Brazilian wax, but which I'm hoping is a meal. Villa Bella is a seaside town not in the mould of what you'd expect from the Brazilian coastline. Not a particularly eye-catching beach, no soft drinks concessions, no sun umbrellas, no six-pack-clad dudes working out on the sand and no local girls showing off their legendary South American derrieres. There doesn't seem to be much in the way of beachfront entertainment either – it seems to be one of those seaside towns which is more town than seaside. It's Hove to Brighton's Copacabana.

We drive through a nexus of fairly rundown streets, featuring motor parts shops and local eateries that would take some personal courage to enter; the drooling Rottweiler at the entrance being the most welcoming member of staff. The town is ramshackle, scruffy and a bit untidy, but it has a certain ugly duckling charm. And with young kids happily playing football on the street – no doubt preparing to thrash England at the 2030 World Cup – and with mums hanging their washing on lines while exchanging the latest gossip, this place does feel like a community and there's a warmth in not only the temperature. We reach her sister's house. It is a tired-looking, small, white building, accessed via a narrow iron door and up a flight of stairs. The myriad gates, spikes and bars on the windows in this town betray the darker side of Brazilian life.

Sheyla rings the doorbell. Her sister answers and greets her with a hug. She and Sheyla are very alike, but she looks altogether more real and sensible. Siblings are often a useful way of gauging just how much plastic surgery someone has had, as they are by definition a control in the experiment – a walking 'before' photograph. Her sister's softly weathered face suggests that all her time is taken up with a job, being

a mother and being a wife. A glance at Sheyla's face doesn't tell you anything, because like the rest of her, it isn't hers. These are two siblings that have demonstrably taken different paths in life.

I'm invited to sit and enjoy a coffee from a flask. I'm told the coffee is a fine-ground variety of Brazil's finest, boiled and left to settle, after which sugar is added. Flying across the Americas and changing various time zones has left my head feeling like it left my body weeks ago, so the coffee is a welcome elixir. I needn't have bothered – Sheyla is a walking stimulant. We've been in the house for five minutes and she strides back into the living room, wearing a different, dazzling outfit. I am to learn that she changes outfits more often than Beyonce at an awards ceremony. She is clutching a variety of medicinal-looking empty plastic sacks and tubes. These are her implants. The secrets of her success, the tools of her trade. And they look nearly as awful inside someone as out. She has saline implants – essentially salt-water-filled plastic bags. There is a little valve in each implant which a tube is inserted into, through which the solution can be squeezed, allowing you to inflate to a degree you are comfortable with. Sheyla is comfortable with an uncomfortable amount. Currently her breasts contain 4000 centilitres of fluid per breast. But this isn't enough, apparently.

'So if you have these implants filled up to the brim, how big will that make you per breast?' I ask.

Sheyla, matter of fact, says, 'I will be 5,500 per breast.'

'Will that make you the holder of the title, the number one biggest implants in the world?'

'Yeah, if I fill 5,500 each one that will make me the large implants in the world.'

'Really? Number one?'

'Number one of the whole entire world,' she says, like a wide-eyed contestant in a beauty pageant. Her English is pretty good, but not perfect and has some idiosyncrasies, including making her sound quite childlike.

'And how would that make you feel to be number one?'

'Yeah I always wanna be remembered so every time the people remember about breast implants, they got to remember of me.'

'Is that important to you, that you go down in history, that you will have a legacy?'

'Yeah. I did this for my ego, to be happy, to be remember, so that in only a little bit more time, I will be ready to stop. But I wanna keep my size for at least a year or two, because I want to have fun with that, I wanna have a lot of fun with my breasts,' she declares bouncily.

I'm not sure what it means exactly. But it's illustrative of the fact that Sheyla comes across as implicitly comical, and speaks, I think unintentionally, in comical sound-bites. At regular intervals, she refers to her adoration of Dolly Parton, which seems appropriate, as there is obviously something quite bouncy, comical and not entirely real about our Dolly either. But because of her heavy Brazilian accent she tends to chop the ends off quite a few words, and regularly announces, often with a tear in her eye, 'I just love Dolly Part. I want to be Dolly Part. Dolly Part is so beautiful and I want to be her.'

'So you are going to be a world record breaker for a year or two, make a bit of money?' I ask.

'Yeah.'

This is an unconvincing response. She is clearly not lacking business nous but something tells me fame is the bigger prize. Though somewhat manufactured, her airport arrival felt like the kind of thing she lives for. Already I have the sense that while Minka's large breasts were solely about making money and indulging her husband sexually, Sheyla's breasts seem to be about her, and the persona she's constructed. We move upstairs for the long-promised barbeque. We eat on the top floor which has a roof and a floor, but no outer walls. Quite a feat of engineering, though not intentional I think. It looks like a part of the house which hubby hasn't had enough bank holidays to complete, much to his wife's chagrin. Every man has a bit of his home he hasn't finished. It's worn by all of us as a badge of pride. This man's unfinished bit is an entire storey of the building – more power to his elbow.

The open nature of this top floor provides a vantage point over the whole city, which is bigger from on high that it looks in the back of a Fiat Punto taxi. The barbeque delivers.

It's decidedly un-British – not a burnt Taste The Difference sausage in sight. Just soft, sumptuous meat that would have the most ardent vegetarians reconsidering their position. A variety of just bloody enough lamb and beef, alongside some freshly broiled ham expertly grilled by a family friend. He has the air of someone who is inexplicably always there, even though there isn't really a reason for him to be there, rather like a badly written sitcom character. There were a flurry of Seventies sitcoms that seemed to feature a policeman sitting at the table, drinking tea. For no apparent reason. But this particular gentleman at Sheyla's sister's place is a bone fide alpha male and he strikes me as someone it would be nice to have around, in any house, at any time. A man who understands how to cook dead animal, who knows how to hang a hook that will stay up and how to recalibrate the engine on a Mark 4 Volkswagon Golf. A proper, actual, man man. Now you're talking.

As we delve into this protein fest, Sheyla noticeably strains with her back.

'Do you ever get a bad back?' I ask.

'Yeah my back pain. The pain is a lot. Before never hurt, but now they hurt. So when I go to a restaurant like now I just rest my boobs on the table.'

I pull a face of surprise. 'Really?'

At which point there plays out one of those moments that I will take to my grave. Like shaking hands with the smallest

man on Earth, or hugging someone called Dennis who has turned himself into a cat, it's pretty amazing. I am watching a woman rest her breasts on the table in order to rest her back. It's an utterly bizarre act of comedy, and practicality. And it raises the key themes so far in my encounter with Sheyla – hilarity, and a sense of – what the hell are you doing to yourself? There was a hardiness about Minka, a resolve that made her look like a pro when it came to carrying her accessories around. It's just business. With Sheyla, the whole enterprise feels more impulsive and emotional and I'm not sure that she, or her back, will take the strain for long.

After eating almost an entire farmyard's worth of barbequed animal, it is time to hit the mall, and time for part two of the Sheyla show. She insists on bringing her make-up artist and close friend, a detail which indicates what this visit will entail, and she doesn't disappoint. At the entrance to the mall a small crowd gather, taking pics and staring. After many minutes, we enter the shopping centre itself and Sheyla tends to her fame the way you are supposed to tend to a log fire – enjoy the heat when it's roaring, and stoke it up a bit when it goes down. In those brief moments when nobody is taking an interest, Sheyla shrieks, giggles and if all that fails, wiggles her breasts.

Let's be clear about this – there's no irony being deployed. No Babs Windsor tongue firmly in cheek, with a wink to the knowing audience. Sheyla is just simply wiggling her breasts so people will look at her. End of, as an indigenous Londoner would say. Look at me, I'm wiggling my breasts. *Look!* Wiggle wiggle wiggle! It goes without saying, it's unedifying, but I guess this is what you do if you have no discernible skill and if fame is the game. Sheyla has made herself unique in a way nature failed to do. Paul McCartney was born with the power of melody, Picasso the power of the paintbrush and Shakespeare was good at plays. With no such obvious gifts, or the education or opportunities to realise any talents lying dormant in her, what's a girl who wants to be a star to do?

Amid the mostly positive public reaction to Sheyla's arrival, there is a black sheep in the adoring family. A middle-aged woman utters some remark about her being ugly. This woman is in a group of one saying it, but isn't there a silent majority, even the people snapping Sheyla on their mobiles, who also think that what she has become is ugly? Because let's be honest – it is – isn't it? The passing party-pooper is surely just the less deceived in this whole affair, and the more honest of her fellow shoppers. Sheyla's reaction to the heckle is characteristically ebullient.

'What do you think about that?' I say. 'She called you ugly. That's not very nice is it?'

'She is old, she is old, she is unfashionable.' I'm chuckling at Sheyla's brass. It's a great line. Even if it doesn't actually answer the question. I push the issue.

'It's got to hurt a little bit, hasn't it?'

She pushes her head back haughtily. 'Just make me laugh,' she says. Reaching for another, more on-message passer-by, she says, 'Look, she say I am beautiful.'

'Oh well, that's better isn't it,' I say. 'You love this, don't you, you know, you are running after people and helping them with the camera and showing yourself off.'

'Yes, you know, because I like the attention, it's good for me.'

Is attention really good for anyone? I personally think you're damned if you don't get it, but double damned if you do. This is a problem Sheyla seems to desperately want. She suddenly grabs my arm and frogmarches me to our next photo opportunity, at a swimwear shop. I'm beginning to eel somewhat compromised at this point. My interviewee is driving this whole thing. Should I be a bit worried, um, you know, journalistically? I have travelled many thousands of miles, I have a limited amount of time with my subject, and I need to understand why she has made these choices in her life. But this seems unlikely to happen because when I turn my back for three seconds, I discover she has squeezed into a bikini designed for a five-year-old and is dancing around inside the shop, declaring, 'I like my boobies. And I love Dolly Part.'

Any sense of control I might have goes out the window at this point. It is the Sheyla show, and I only have a walk-on part. I tell myself I'll have to go with this, as the public Sheyla is an unstoppable hurricane of publicity and excitement. I

will wait for the doors to close and the smile to drop before probing any more deeply. Until then I'll have to just enjoy one of my top ten most insane visits to a shopping mall. And incongruously spot a pair of flipflops that would suit my wife.

On the way out, I put it to Sheyla that the interest from the public is surely in her breasts and not actually her. Isn't that a bit odd? I ask her.

'Well,' she says. 'They love my personality. My personality is beautiful.'

'But if your personality is so beautiful why do you need these?' I point pointedly to her pointy breasts.

'These is just a complement, just a complement,' she explains. 'These are my diamonds, my accessories.'

At this point, Sheyla is distracted, like Tiger Woods at a waitress convention. She starts conversing with another insta-group of 'fans' and then comes to me with a summing up of their brief but intense discussion.

'They say I have to go bigger!'

'Oh really?' I reply. 'This is how you make big decisions is it?'

The irony of this statement is missed on Sheyla and she carries on into the distance, tottering, jiggling and wiggling. This isn't someone who does self-aware.

Once the dust has settled, Sheyla and I break every health and safety rule in the book by going to have a sit down on the local beach. I want to get her away from the crowds and

talk to the real Sheyla about how she became Sheyla with a capital S. The sun is beginning to set, and it coats us both in a warm yellow light. Sheyla looks even more tanned, I just look slightly jaundiced. Sheyla is tired - this suits her - at last she's calm and somewhat manageable. Riding the crest of this wave, I actually ask her a question.

'So how did you get to this point of all these operations and looking the way you do now?'

'I came from a very, very poor family,' she explains. 'You know, after my dad died, my mum had eleven kids and she was sick, and she couldn't take care of all of us and I wanted to kill myself. I took some rat medicine that will kill you, I drunk that.'

Eh? Have you ever heard a sentence so packed with incident? This is a lot to take in. Only characters in soap operas talk like that don't they? (e.g. 'I had the abortion because Terry wasn't the father who killed Norm who's gone to Australia because he sold the shipyard to Uncle Phil who isn't actually anyone's uncle'). But this is how Sheyla talks. It's very, very troubling stuff indeed, but the way she reels it off makes it feel like another performance. This time it's 'sad Sheyla'. Maybe I'm being too harsh. I give her the benefit of the doubt. Unhelpfully I'm growing fond of this crazy lady.

'Rat poison. You consumed rat poison?' I say.

'Yes, rat poison and I drunk all this medication and I guess it was because all this happened to me at first.'

At which point she takes out her leopard-skin encased iPhone to show me pictures of herself before any of the plastic surgery. She does look wildly different. Mousey brown hair, an innocent, slightly freckled face, shy-looking, big eyes, but no big boobs. It's a different person. But not necessarily a worse one.

'Do you think that is me, the same person?' she asks.

'I would never in a million years think that was you,' I say.

'Do you want me to look like this?' she continues, warming to her theme. Why am I accountable for her actions all of a sudden? Leave me out of this – I wasn't there at the time! Sheyla has a dangerous habit of asking near strangers to lend credence to her drastic actions and life choices.

'Well, I think, you know, you looked pretty in a different way then,' I suggest.

'I wasn't happy. You know, if I was like this right now I would just break the mirror.'

'Really?'

'Yeah, not happy,' she says.

At this point there is a rare flash of sincerity in Sheyla's eyes. She means it. She seems to truly dislike her former self. It doesn't take a great deal of psychological Cluedo to work out that the girl in the photograph was in a bad place, and one way to fix the problem was to change the way she looked and thus change her life. In a sense it's using the surgeon's

knife to force life's hand. This I suspect is the core hope at the heart of most plastic surgery patients. As I am to discover later, plastic surgery is rarely rational – this is one of the great myths about it.

The wind is blowing Sheyla's bleached, crunchy, yellow doll's hair. We get to the turning-point moment in her life. When she was twenty she met an Englishman who changed everything. Who was, you guessed it, a big boob fanatic. Ah, the smoking gun ...

'He saved my life,' she begins, 'because after that, I never ever tried to hurt myself, only love myself.'

'Did he originally suggest that you get implants?'

'No, he did not say that I need to, but he say he love big breast woman. If I have implants he will be happy because he loves huge breasts.'

Right ...

'Is he a big boob fanatic?'

'Yeah. When I met him all his computer, magazine, full of porn stars like all these huge breast woman.'

What a lovely start to a relationship. 'Hey mum, I've met this guy, he's really nice – he's got a job, he's nice looking. And he has a massive collection of hardcore pornography featuring women with gargantuan breasts.'

She goes on. 'He was lot fanatic. When I met him I didn't know, I didn't know Minka, I didn't know Maxi Mound and then he introduced me all these woman, he say would you

like to be like that and then I was thinking to myself yeah, that's pretty.'

'Are you sure you didn't do it just to make him happy because that's how it is in a relationship, you want to make your partner happy?'

'No. I wanna make him happy and me happy because if he was happy I was happy. But I love my breasts because I'm not with him any more and I still love my breasts so it wasn't really about him.'

'So you think that having these operations, having big breasts has saved your life?' I ask.

'Yes. Saved my life. Because look at me how happy I am.'

Now, at this point I should say I have a rule of thumb - people who say 'Look how happy I am' aren't happy. The revelation here is that, as with Minka, there is a man, a big boob fanatic, who has instigated this whole process. It's impossible to imagine that Sheyla's life would have played out like this if she hadn't met this Englishman (what is it about Englishmen by the way? I'm not proud). Clearly he met her at a time when she was genuinely vulnerable and he was no doubt rather caring and loving and whatever he gave her emotionally hit the spot, and perhaps even saved her life. But his affection came with a price tag. 'I like massive breasts ...' I'm imagining the conversation went. '... Here's a phone number of a great plastic surgeon I know. Oh and by the way, I love you.' No pressure then.

What's curious though, and why I'm prepared to not judge this man too harshly is that clearly Sheyla has embraced the change her body has forced upon her. He has long since bitten the dust, but the legacy of his fetish lives on in this woman. She has taken the big boobs and run with them, so to speak. With Sheyla, there isn't that sense of someone who foolishly tattooed the name of a lover onto their chin, only to discover they've run off with someone else. Rather, this crazy and in my view appalling intervention from the hand of the surgeon, caused Sheyla to restart her life. A reboot. With the reboobs. A reboob reboot. OK, that's enough.

And so we are where we are. This is Sheyla's life now and she doesn't have a sense of imprisonment in her own body that Minka does. Minka's boobs are a necessary evil. 'It's money. Money, power,' as she told me over and over again. Sheyla needs the boobs. They are a life support system. The day she had her first op was the first day that she decided for the first time to like herself. So naturally one consequence, and this is the plastic surgery trap, is that to have that feeling, you'll inevitably go back for more. Before we depart the beach, which is now lit only by the moon, and passing police cars, she calls her plastic surgeon on the phone. It's a jovial chat. It's like she's talking to her hairdresser. She has decided she wants to have her procedure an hour earlier tomorrow. I'm shocked at the informal nature of the chat she's having with this very important man.

I bid her farewell and she goes off for some beauty sleep, prior to having some beauty inflicted on her by a surgeon's blade. I'm surprised to learn that neither her sister or indeed any of her family will be in attendance tomorrow. I return to Sheyla's sister's house for another sweet coffee, to find out why. Sadly barbeque boy isn't there. He's probably broiling meat and installing hooks in someone else's house. I ask her how she feels about her baby sister's plans. I feel I already know the answer.

'I am really worried about not only me but the whole family is worried about it,' she says. 'Because it becomes an obsession, a huge obsession for her and we really don't like that to become a health problem, and nowadays going to a surgery for her is just the same as going to have her nails done, so I really don't like it. I don't wanna be like partner with her, when something bad comes up, so I don't go to the surgeries with her any more.'

This is a tragic revelation. To see how someone can hurt others so much, by hurting themselves. Sheyla is far from the only victim. And her sister is across all the issues Sheyla is oblivious to, or in denial of, namely the considerable risks attached to what she is doing.

'It really seems to upset you what she is doing to herself,' I say. 'How hard is it for you to see this?'

'It is very hard actually, it makes all of us very sad indeed. We all like, we get sad but there is nothing we can do, we get sad.'

Morning has broken and I'm feeling slightly emotionally hungover from the madness of the previous day. As I push bits of hotel breakfast around my plate, I mull over the irony that today is Sheyla's 'special day', when really, special is the last word I'd use. Sometimes when I'm in these situations, I feel I should make some kind of intervention. Like maybe when I'm in the operating theatre, I should rugby tackle the anaesthetist to the floor prior to the op. It's like those cameramen and women who film a zebra being stalked by a hungry lion. Don't they sometimes want to put the camera down and shout 'He's behind you!'?

But above and beyond asking her countless times what the hell she's thinking and saying 'Don't do this!', I don't feel I can go any further. No more so than I could do with my own sister. Ultimately she is a sovereign individual and she's mistress of her own destiny. And if her own family can't stop her, then what hope for me? Arriving at the swanky plastic surgery clinic where she is to be pumped up, I go up to meet Sheyla in her hospital bedroom. She's dressed in a plain white bed gown – as dressed-down as you'll ever see this woman. I kiss her on both cheeks and ask her how she's feeling. She clearly hasn't had much sleep and her face is puffy. I recall my chat with her sister the night before.

'She is obviously quite upset about you know, your operations,' I say.

'I don't listen to anyone except myself and I don't like people try to change me. People who try to change me I just keep away, them away from me.'

'Even the people who really care about you like your family?' I ask.

'Even the people who care about me because is all about me, I know what I am doing and I happy to do what I am doing. That is why I wanna go bigger, because I want to be bigger, I wanted to break the world record, that makes me happy. I think my breasts is the most beautiful thing I have on my body and as long as I am awake I am going to keep them, keep growing.'

We are interrupted by a nurse coming in to give Sheyla a pill of some sort. This last exchange is typical of what I have learned about her. She is driven, an unstoppable force, her mind uncluttered with concern for the upset she is causing to those around her. This is not to be harsh about Sheyla. This is something she is sincere about having to do. It is a compulsion. This is genuinely what she wants and has to do. Whether she should be allowed to do it is another question. Her plastic surgeon is no doubt the best money can buy, but I ask myself whether she could go as big as she's about to, in America or Britain; I'm not sure it would happen. Brazil is number two in the world for the most plastic surgeries behind the USA, but here the range of what you can have done, and to what extent, is greater.

As for today, it isn't just her breasts that she is having fiddled with. She is also having a chin lift, liposuction and botox. Well, you know, when you drop the car into the garage for a new clutch, you normally ask the mechanic to fix that wonky wing mirror and faulty taillight while he's at it. So what's the difference, right ...?

From the moment Sheyla and I first met, she has been imploring me to go into the operation with her. I'm actually not that squeamish about that kind of thing and have always found all aspects of medicine utterly compelling. I think being a doctor or nurse has to be the closest you'll get jobwise to really making a difference in people's lives. Dead or not dead. Well or not well. That is often the consequence of a medic's day at the office. As Sheyla is wheeled into the theatre, I have the slight concern that, as she is such a force of nature, perhaps she is immune to anaesthetic, and will chat incessantly during the procedure about her boobies and her undying regard for 'Dolly Part'. Fortunately she is not immune and one of the few upsides of this regrettable exercise, is ninety minutes of silence. As tubes pump and machines bleep, I'm struck by the stupid irony that in parts of the world there are no hospital beds for people who need them to carry on living, while elsewhere there are people having ops that are resolutely unnecessary. Maybe I'll be eating my words when I go in for my brow lift in ten years' time ...

So instead of having new implants, Sheyla is having her existing ones filled to capacity. I was shocked at how serious an operation it was. The surgeon cuts right at the lower edge of her areola, that's the round darker circle that circumnavigates the nipple (OK, I can't describe breasts). He essentially slices into what looks like the most tender part of the bosom. It's then flipped open, like the wide round lid on a plastic sports bottle. Visible immediately is the clear bag – the implant. Sheyla looks at this point like a particularly creative drugs mule. The salty water is injected into the implant via the narrow tube Sheyla was waving around in front of me the previous day. At this point the areola is flapped down again and stitched up. Ow.

I make my way out of the theatre and head to the canteen for a tea and a plain biscuit. I feel like I've been operated on. I wait for Sheyla to come round. I then hear that the operation was OK and that she is now a world record holder. Officially the most enhanced woman in the world. Clutching the best bunch of flowers a Brazilian petrol station has to offer, I head to her room. As I open the door, as always with Sheyla, it's not what I'm expecting. She's lying in the bed, bandaged, bruised, groggy. That's understandable. But in the room with her is a photographer with a massive camera, snapping away. He asks her to sit up a bit. 'Look this way. Look that way,' he says. What's going on? Before I get to asking, I greet her with a kiss. I try to be upbeat. She's just had a significant amount surgery and is fragile in every possible way.

'Look at this lady. How are you doing?' I say.

'Is that flowers for me?' she asks sweetly.

'Of course they are for you, who do you think they're for?'

'Oh my God, you did not need to!' she replies.

'Of course! So, who's the photographer?'

'This photographer, he's for my publicity,' she explains, slurring her words from the medication. 'So when I need to tell my story I have those photographs.'

'Are you really in the mood to do publicity?' I say. 'You've just had a major operation.'

Sheyla abruptly barks at the snapper, 'Come on, take some pictures.'

'But you've got, like, bandages on and everything.' She takes no notice of me. It's a macabre scene. She's still got the lines that the surgeon's made with a pen for the lipo. And she's got bandages on her face and yet she's doing press photographs. She's a control freak out of control. I take this opportunity to ask her about the record now.

'So are you the number one now, the world record holder?' I ask.

'As far as I know I'm the world record in breast implants.'

'And how does that feel?' I ask.

'I feel great. I just, I can't be jumpy now cos I just got them done.'

'You can't what?' I ask.

'I just want to jump,' she says.

I wouldn't if I were her.

She then turns to me, Bambi eyes, and says, 'Do they look bigger to you?'

'They do look bigger, yes,' I say diplomatically. I can't tell. They were always too big. And just terrible.

'A lot bigger?'

'Yes, they're even bigger.' There are men the world over having the opposite conversation about their wives' arses. Oh the vagaries of the female psyche.

And still Sheyla seeks the validation of a near stranger.

'Are you sure?' she asks. 'But you see I can add a little bit more.'

'What, another op?' I ask, heart sinking. I'm not hearing this.

'Yes,' she replies.

'More liquid to go in there?' I point to her chest which is now closer to my finger than it was three hours ago.

Sheyla nods.

'I thought this was your last operation, I'm quite surprised to hear there's going to be another one?'

'But I always break promises,' she says brazenly.

'That makes me worried because I think maybe you're going to have these operations forever ...'

'I don't know,' she says. She clearly does.

'But are you going to ever ... sort of, you know, say enough is enough. To say I'm big enough now and my health is a big priority?'

'Yeah, my health is big priority but I want to be happy with myself. This is gonna be my thirty-second operation.'

'Thirty-second?' I ask. Am I hearing right?

'And I'm still beautiful, I think I'm beautiful. I just ... you saw my picture from before and after. Nobody believed that red, pink dress was this person, a world record is something really big for me. You got to be remembered and I want to be remembered on today.'

I'm trying to decipher how much of this is drug induced. A bit like a barroom chat with Pete Doherty.

She goes on, 'I just want to make my family happy, I don't hurt anybody. Why the hell I have to listen to people, if I'm not happy, why? Do you think I want to try to kill myself again?'

'It strikes me that your breasts have kind of been part of your recovery from depression? You sort of associate your breasts with happiness? Is that right?' I ask.

'Yeah, I'm happy the way I am, I'm happy. I'm really happy. In a way because I want to close my past. I want to forget everything that happening to me. Everything.'

Her declaration of how happy she is arrives at the same time as her tears. Another contradiction in the muddled mind of this remarkable young woman. I'm hugely disappointed

that she is announcing that she'll have yet another operation after this, and for a moment I can feel some flavour of how it must be for her family all the time. Being told one thing, only for another thing to actually happen. Sheyla is a rollercoaster. Spending time with her is like being on that rollercoaster. It makes you queasy, shocked, hysterical and at all times you have a trickle of anxiety in the pit of your stomach. The large breasts in Sheyla's case are, as I said, not rational, which is why I found her story even more sad that that of Minka. Yes Sheyla has some fame, and she certainly makes more money than she would if she was stacking shelves at the Brazilian equivalent of Morrisons.

And who am I and who is anyone to tell her to be 'normal', 'ordinary', 'average' and have the poverty that often accompanies that? She has, through sheer force of personality and two large breasts, willed a career and a livelihood for herself. I enjoyed my time with Sheyla and, like lots of things that aren't good for you, I liked her. I wonder about her future hopes for love. Any kind of relationship with this woman, even mild friendship, would be bad for the blood pressure, but like that slice of streaky bacon, probably worth shortening your life slightly for. I hope someone nice has the years to spare. And the energy. And the patience. And he's got to like large breasts ...

Curiously, as I look back on my experience of this world, all of these women cut the figure of a tragic heroine. There's a strange mix of courage and vulnerability displayed in their booming figures. It's a gauntlet thrown down to the world. 'Look at me! Be mesmerised by me. Look at how much power I harness over both all of mankind, and myself.' Indeed to the big boob fanatics, these women are like goddesses. Semi-fictional deities. But I'm not a big boob fan, and I looked into the dark underbelly of these goddesses. I saw the literal and metaphorical shadow cast by these women's breasts. And it wasn't pretty. Sheyla's done this to her body, because, bluntly, she's screwed up. This was her crazy solution. In a sense it worked, because she's still here. And she has made a career of it. But she who lives by the large breast will die by it. I'm struck by how it might be for Sheyla when her body is her last loved one to say no. To construct an entire personality around a certain set of physical attributes whacks of a deal with the devil. Or at least with the plastic surgeon.

These women I met and other myriad large-chested women I came into contact with in this unique world, all had certain things in common. A deep strength, a will, a drive, a determination, the stuff which I certainly lack, and I think the majority of us do, to that level. They are hellbent on their various goals, goals which are hardwired into their souls; whether it's to make a career, be famous, noticed, rich or just to please their fetishistic partner. There's also in all of them a sense with this surgery, and their new vulgar-fraction figures, of a line drawn in the sand with their past. Whether by the manipulation of someone else or a genuine desire to make a new start, all these women have closed a chapter in their early life, with the help of a pragmatic (that's a kind word) plastic surgeon. But it's a strange thing to do to make money or to make a man, or thousands of men, love you. There are surely other ways to get those things, that 99.999 per cent of us opt for. There are just so few women who will butcher, pervert and stretch to near breaking point their own bodies, to achieve a given end. None of these women had, in my view, a sense of the sanctity of their own bodies. Something most people are born with. In these women, it's absent. It has to be - look at the pictures! There's something implicitly brutal about the sheer size of these fake boobs. As I said before, it looks painful. You look at these pictures of all these women and you just say Noooo. Even Jordan, like the British economy, has shrunk drastically in recent times.

It's a unique woman that will sacrifice every aspect of her quality of life to look a certain way. And I realise that's why my far-flung journeys are more than just a chance to sample different airlines' complimentary snacks (though let's not underplay this too - I personally favour some kind of nut selection over, say, the mini pretzl). The choices these women have made are utterly alien to most of us. And so why do they do it, when we won't? This is the question I am burning a new hole in the ozone layer to find out. My early footsteps tell me a variety of factors coalesce to produce women like Minka and Sheyla. We know about the shadowy male figures, and no one's impervious to the lure of dollars. But perhaps most importantly, there's something in these women that is scarred, long before they ever saw a plastic surgeon. There is a sense that all of these women are slightly damaged individuals. Fragile souls with not just low self-esteem, but an almost nonexistent one. The breasts strike me as buffers against a world that might have hurt them in the past. They are airbags, weapons, wands, sandbags. Two massive defence mechanisms that will literally stop anyone getting close to them ever again.

Which brings me to my next extraordinary journey. What if your body is an entire *7 ft 9 in* defence mechanism that you were born with? A body that scares men away and can make daily life an unedifying struggle. Meet the tallest women in the world...

CHAPTER 2

The World's Tallest Woman and Me

PART 1

'Why are they staring at me?'
Ellen Bayer and Sandy Allen's story

I am 6 ft 5 in, but I don't feel tall. I never have. I don't have the brain of a tall person, the mentality of a tall person and I don't have any of the baggage that goes with being tall. I just don't *feel* tall. It's an odd one. I don't have a kinship with other tall people, and there's nothing therapeutic about being in a room with a bunch of other tall folk. In fact I look at tall people and think of them as different to me. Now this might be denial – after all, I am pretty damn tall. But I think it stems from the fact that height came to me very late in life. Throughout my childhood, and into my early teens, I was average or just above average height. I spent many years being normal height. It's not like, in the school photo aged ten, I towered over my nearest colleagues. I was never recruited to join the school basketball team, or go in goal for football. In fact I was so underwhelming as a young footballer, I usually got the job of linesman – thereby safely guaranteeing no actual access to the ball.

It wasn't until about the age of fifteen that I started to get taller, and not stop. But still it was fairly gradual. It is said you don't stop growing until you are twenty-one, but I think I was still putting on height on the eve of my thirtieth birthday. So as a tall person, I was a late developer, it being bestowed upon me when I was old enough to handle it, like the height equivalent of being made to wait for a hefty inheritance. I am very grateful for this, as over all those years in which I formed my character and defined myself, as little people are wont to do, I did it with a body that was variously 5 ft 5 in, 5 ft 6 in, 5 ft 7 in, etc. It's a different ball game if you are 6 ft at the age of fourteen. I was spared this, and the inevitable baggage that goes with it. The knowledge that clothes shopping would be an angst-ridden and fruitless endeavour. The permanent, ingrained slouch that comes from years of talking to shorties. The sense of awkwardness and gawkishness that comes from towering over people from a young age. I think tall people feel like they are taking up space, they are getting in the way. There's something untidy about a massively tall teenager.

When height came, the way it manifested itself was very specific. My height is all about my legs. My legs are massively long. I am a normal male, with very common or garden proportions, but I'm on stilts. Hence I don't have the wan, elongated features of a massively tall man. I don't have a long, tall person's face, no bony, tall person's fingers, no long Peter Shilton arms, and no long, meandering tall person's ears. Often, if I meet people sitting down – and I do love a good sit down – they will be astonished when I stand up. My face and body betray none of my considerable, actual stature. From hip bone to shoulder, you're looking at the same length as that of a 5 ft 10 in male, but it's a different story from the hip bone down. And thus we come to the core gripe of all tall people – clothes. Now as I've explained exhaustively, from belt upwards, sizing has never been a problem, but with a 36 inch inside leg, trousers are a bit of a headache. Very fortunately Levis 501s came in this size, which in the 1990s was important as they were the jeans you wore, but that was about it. All the trousers I've had since around 1994 have been essentially too small for me.

I feel fortunate to be tall and don't have any hangups about it. I think as a man, whenever the height comes, it's no real burden to carry. A longer back, in many cases, means good posture is more of a premium, and a lanky male will probably never prosper on a rugby field. But otherwise, being tall converges quite comfortably with what society deems a 'man' to be. Being tall, as well as being broad, well built, a bit hairy and having a deep voice, these are – perhaps

irrationally – the predefined qualities of an alpha male. Don't get me wrong, there's nothing more alpha male than a three-foot-wide prop forward who barely comes up to my waist. But societally, we do associate bigness, and thus, height with masculinity. What's the Mills & Boon cliché of the archetypal man? Tall, dark and handsome.

There are logistical issues with being tall, for example I did have one or two girlfriends who were very petite and I do remember suggesting we sit down a lot. There is also the slight concern that a longer back could prove problematic later in life, anatomically. There is the problem of entering doorways in period homes, and in a group that's up to no good, the tall person will be spotted first, and thus brought to account, while the smaller characters have managed to squirrel themselves away in time. This prejudice notwithstanding, being a tall male, I would suggest, doesn't really present you with a crisis of identity. It doesn't jar with the boundaries by which we define a man, but rather supports them.

Not so, alas, with females. In an almost mirror-opposite of how we define masculinity, women, in the words of society, are delicate flowers, petite and ladylike. Women aren't expected to be very short, of course not, but even the smallest female will doubtless encounter fewer mental obstacles than their male equivalent. Napoleon, anyone? But to be very tall and female? Well, unless you are a catwalk model, it's tricky. Ask your average woman over six feet in height and she will be none so romantic about her situation. Very tall females I've met complain particularly about not feeling feminine. It's remarkable, because what could be more feminine than legs that go on forever, long slim arms and an overall statuesque presence? One such person who doesn't feel feminine is Ellie. She's a member of the Central Arizona Tall Society. It's where my journey starts, to meet the tallest woman on the planet. I'm on an airplane right now, filling up my builder's tea reserves and watching *You Don't Mess with the Zohan*, the surprisingly amusing Adam Sandler comedy. Happy days.

My jet experiences the rare occurrence of passing through deep grey cloud as it lands in Arizona. Dots of water on my window tell me something even more surprising. It's raining. In Arizona. Something that, reliably, week in, week out, never happens. I have literally brought the weather with me. It's disappointing, because the one thing I was looking forward to about Arizona was blindingly bright sunshine and a gloriously dry heat. Not today. The tens of thousands of pensioners who flock here from the damp East Coast to see out their days won't need to feel too homesick today. It's drizzly and grey. The things that most likely drove them here in the first place – namely asthma, psoriasis, seasonally adjusted syndrome and a feeling of always being a bit cold – will be returning to them with a vengeance on this decidedly British day.

But here's another thing the Americans don't do: gloomy. And as I arrive at my hotel, which is where the Central Arizona Tall Society's annual bash is actually taking place, the receptionist is so friendly, you'd think it was the sunniest day of the year. She greets my arrival like I am the official from the Lottery company, personally delivering her cheque. In fact, I'm taking one of the 153 bedrooms on the grounds of her workplace, and I'm paying $89. I ditch my unfeasibly full backpack in my room; I have no idea how to pack and always bring too much of one item every time. For this trip it's toothpaste - four tubes - why? And way too many socks. Though having just arrived and being in the mood to sit lazily on my bed, with my shoes and coat still on, watching an old episode of *I Love Lucy*, I have received an invitation to the arrival party of the tall club. This is the party before the party. Which I think is overkill. I am similarly not keen on weddings that involve dinners on the eve of the big day and elaborate post-wedding breakfasts, then an inaugural lunch, then wind-down drinks. Oh and by the way we're all going on the honeymoon! Enough already ...

However, I don't want to put any noses out of joint at the Tall Society, even though I probably lack the reach required to do so with this bunch. I'm feeling jaded and a bit scruffy after nine hours of air travel, time zone changes and Adam Sandler. I comfort myself with the knowledge that this encounter shouldn't be too bruising, as for once I'm not the outsider entering a quirky world. They are tall people, there to celebrate people who are tall. And I am tall. Very tall, really, even if I don't feel it. So this will take some screwing up.

I walk over towards the convention centre and spot a tall man digging his luggage out of his luxury sedan. Is he with us? I'm not sure. He's tall. But is he Central Arizona Tall Society tall? What is the tipping point of height, that makes you feel the need to drive, or even fly, many miles to party with other tall people? I'd say 6 ft 8 in. But then I would say that, as I'm the best part of 6 ft 5 in tall! But for me, that would seem to be the kind of height that I suspect becomes impossible to ignore. The kind of height that turns heads in the street, where it's the only talking point at the supermarket checkout when you're buying your spuds. 'Is it snowing up there? Did you fall asleep in the greenhouse?' Etc., etc.

Gathered around the pool near the convention hall are a group of unmistakably and universally tall people. Massive men, who are a head taller than me, and women of the same or similar height to me. I greet them all warmly, receiving reassuringly firm handshakes from the guys, so much as to say 'you're one of us – welcome'. And I receive approving air kisses from the tall women who, I'm guessing, have a preference for tall men. Walking into the convention hall itself, I feel pats on my back and a sea of almost ceiling height smiles. I've come home, it seems. I didn't know I had left home. But now I'm back. There are an array of tall people –

young men, older beer-bellied men, glamorous young ladies and one or two plain but friendly women of a certain age. I try to sign in with one such lady, her height diluted by the fact that she is sitting down, though she has a tall face which acts as a hint to the rest of her. She has a bureaucratic air and explains dryly that I must be measured before signing in. Suddenly I'm worried. Will I make the cut? Has my claim of being tall got legs?

An avuncular man in his fifties, bespectacled and wearing a shiny blue baseball jacket (the likes of which I haven't seen since the late 1980s when they were all the rage in North London), takes me in hand and conducts the measurement. The crowd turn to watch the procedure. It feels like an initiation ceremony, and I'm starting to feel hunted, like a pig that's suddenly realised why he's been receiving such rich dinners all these years.

'You're six foot four and a half,' he declares. Slightly shorter than I had thought. Am I about to be found out? I've been pretending to be tall all these years, dining out on it, always getting to sit in the front for every car journey, and engendering no small amount of sympathy from fellow airplane passengers when I squeeze into my economy seat. And it's all been a sham. I'm a small little fucker. Who knew!

Helplessly, I turn to the wall of high faces studying me and ask, 'So, am I in? Am I in?'

There follows a pause you could drive a Greyhound bus through, at which point they shout: 'Yes.' There is a spontaneous round of applause. This is a very happy moment. I belong. And I can enter this society, as a fully paid-up member. I thank them, and begin to work the room, exchanging stories, all of them tall. Amid the gathered throng, one person stands out from the crowd, literally head and shoulders above the rest. A fair-haired young woman, perhaps thirty years of age and astonishingly tall. I gasp. And I'm not a big gasper. But I do gasp. Her shoulder-length blonde hair, shy, evasive eyes and awkward smile give her an almost Lady Diana air, circa 1986. It's Ellen Bayer. As I proceed towards her, the closer I get, the more I have to crane my head upwards. This is a new experience for me, and I instantly sympathise with my aforementioned, diminutive suitors. What they went through, and for why!

Ellen's upper body floats around at such an inconceivable height, above this already lofty crowd, it gives the impression she is an elongated genie floating gaseously above her bottle. Somewhere, up high, testing my eyesight to its already strained limits, is a warm and friendly face.

'Hello,' I say. 'I'm Mark.'

I reach up to shake her hand. I'm reminded of the character of Al in the *Police Squad* comedy series. Al, played by the seven-foot actor Ronald 'Tiny Ron' Taylor, is a character so tall you only ever see his upper body on camera, and

never his face. It's probably my favourite *Police Squad* sight gag. Ellen is almost tall enough to play that iconic character herself.

'Hi, I'm Ellen. Good to meet you.'

I cut to the chase.

'So Ellen, how tall are you?'

'I'm six foot ten,' she replies matter of factly.

'Six ten - OK ... I've got to say one thing I've always dreamed of doing, never been able to until this moment is to hug a woman that is taller than me. Would you indulge me in a hug?'

This could go one of two ways. But I'm feeling lucky. After all, I'm one of her species now. It says so on the badge I'm proudly wearing. The gamble pays off. She smiles and says 'sure'.

I haven't thought this through. My head comes to the same height as her breasts. I've embarked upon the kind of tactile embrace that would make even a bride blush on her honeymoon. Fuck. There's no backing out at this stage. What kind of unspoken social carnage would ensue if I abruptly backed off and said, 'Actually, on second thoughts, no thanks.' Particularly as all of my manoeuvres seem to be attracting the attention of a wider, tall audience. New boy is on probation, and it's too early into what could be an uncomfortably long weekend to put a foot wrong. I plough on with the hug. And it is a faintly supernatural experience. My head lands in the middle of her chest and her long arms wrap around me like two branches of a magically animated tree. And she is strong. So tight is her grip, my glasses are pushed over my nose and to one side of my face, provoking an unintentional moment of Eric Morcambesque high comedy. It's quite the most profound role reversal experience I've ever had. I have no idea whether it's nice as I'm in a flux. It's like trying to work out whether you are enjoying that ice cream, while riding a 100-foot rollercoaster. And like a rollercoaster, it comes to a sudden end after what has felt like an age.

'Thank you so much!' I say. 'Wow, thank you!' I'm hysterical at this point.

'You're welcome,' she says calmly. I suspect my bull in a china shop approach has been a refreshing change from the usual stares and whispers. She seems to respond to my rather direct approach to the issue of her height. With the hug out of the way and a major box ticked in terms of things done in my life, we proceed to a less physical analysis of her size.

'So Ellen, do you think of yourself as tall?' I say. 'Because, actually, I don't.'

'No I don't,' she replies.

'No? You're just you?' I ask, rhetorically.

'Yes, I'm like why's everyone staring at me? And them I'm like "Oh, yeah, that's why",' she says.

'And what are the advantages of your considerable height?'

'I love it when I'm in a crowd or when I'm at a bar and everyone's like this height,' she demonstrates with her hand what she perceives to be the height of 'normal' people; she has to reach down exaggeratedly low to do this. 'And they can't see, and *I* can see for miles.' She smiles at the very thought of this. I'm glad she's so upbeat about it; I was worried this journey into the world of extreme female height might be a bit of a wake. 'Yes that's lovely,' I say, offering nothing.

'That's really nice,' she goes on.

'And is it good at concerts as well?' I ask. 'And in church?' I add, half joking.

'Yes like at concerts, people are like, "Hey, get off the chair." And I'm standing on the ground!'

All this is well and good, but it's the kind of tall small talk that I'm keen to get beyond. I'm not here to gather anecdotes about how hard it is to get a pair of jeans that fit. I am very engaged with the issue of how jarring it is to be so tall and female. I feel here at the Tall Society that for men, such height is a bit of a novelty and if problematic, it is so on a practical everyday level. For women I wondered whether it is an altogether more emotional affliction, affecting self-image, overall confidence and perhaps more importantly the chances of finding love.

As the pre-party comes to a close, I shall hold fire on these issues. It's time for all us tall folk to get into our annoyingly

short beds, feet poking out of the bottom of the duvet, and dream fantastic dreams of airplanes with proper legroom, even in economy. I crash in my strangely bouncy bed and fire up the telly. Irrelevant to whatever level of tiredness, the box always goes on, at least for a few minutes. I enjoy a quick burst of David Letterman's, as always, manifestly perfect topical monologue before passing on the chance of seeing Beyonce Knowles and opting instead for sleep. I am woken at seven by the sound of children shrieking and frolicking in the pool, towards which my bedroom balcony points. I fire up *Good Morning America* and brush my teeth to the sound of a variety of deep voices being right wing. By the sound of it, the world is a terrible place and we need more policemen and soldiers. Dispiriting bile, but less soul destroying than starting the day with a nine-year-old episode of *Everybody Loves Raymond*.

As I sit at breakfast, enjoying what appears to be an eighteen-egg omelette, washed down with a litre of weak coffee, I'm beginning to see the whole tall thing as a darker, sadder issue than I had expected. The atmosphere last night at the pre-party was outwardly jolly and noisy, but tinged with pathos. After all, if you need to have an annual event and set up an all-year-round society – with newsletters, websites and AGMs – doesn't that scream of support group, or even therapy? After all, I don't attend an annual get together of blokes with glasses and uncontrollable hair. So this Tall Society has to be

more than another example of the American love affair with conventions and societies. And it is a love affair. My searches for some of the world's most unique people have been, in the case of America, a bit of a cinch. If there is anything the Americans can base a weekend around, and roll their pick-ups and Winnebagos towards, it will happen. Fat pets, tall people, strong kids - there's an event somewhere, some weekend, somewhere in America in which these uniquities are being celebrated. I'm imagining it's a symptom of America's culture of plurality, in which the individual reigns supreme.

Moreover, America has a strong sense of nationhood, as do all countries that had to fight a war to get their country, post-revolutionary France being another example, but unlike France, America has no sense whatsoever of society. In an echo of Margaret Thatcher's (actually misquoted) comment about there being no such thing as society, in America I feel this to be the case. No real public health service to speak of, a meagre welfare system and a vast proportion of the population both unemployed and unrecognised by the state, it's up to individual groups to roll up their sleeves and create a more localised, federalised sense of belonging. America's self-formed societies, clubs, charities and formal and informal local networks are the glue that holds the country together. Outside of that, the only discernible things that unite the country from East Coast to West are baseball, American football, hamburgers and television.

But this tall club in Arizona is, I think, more than a cultural phenomenon. It is a symbol that being particularly tall is something of an affliction that requires the support and understanding of fellow 'sufferers'. This might be being a bit melodramatic, particularly given that this event is as much as anything a celebration of being tall. But it's clear that it goes beyond having a good old party with some like-minded mates. It is an annual refuge, a chance to feel normal, not be noticed, not be different, and not be asked whether 'it's cold up there'. I'm thus imbued with a sense of sympathy for these people for whom there is no diagnosed medical problem, no disability, no mental disorder, but who still do have something of a daily burden to carry for the way they are born. You could say it sucks. I think it definitely does in Ellen's case; she is perfect in every way - pretty, charming, funny, but just a foot too high. A female that would have had the pick of any number of suitors and be married and bekidded at the time of her choosing, is in fact thirty-nine, single and starting to go beyond the point of hope that something will happen in the love department.

Ellen abruptly announces she and the 'gals' are going shopping for some party clothes for tonight's bash - the 'legendary' Saturday night dinner dance - in which the whole weekend culminates. The theme for tonight is country and western; they strike me as the kind of stalwartly American crowd who wouldn't know any other kind of theme. It's like inviting a bunch of Italian-American gangsters to a 'dark pinstriped suit and spats' themed party; it's effectively *come as you are*. I escort this jaunty rabble of heavily made-up ladies *d'un certain age* to a special shop in Arizona that caters for extra-tall women. There is a noticeable lack of excitement from Ellen about tonight's event – most of the other girls seem up for it, but that's because, as mentioned, they are considerably older than her and have closure romantically, one way or the other. Mostly hovering around the fifty mark, some of them hooked their husbands upwards of two decades ago, and the others – the whiter-haired and wider among them – have accepted that a man arriving now is as likely as the cessation of death and taxes.

Ellen is somewhere in between; she's hopeful and eligible, but tinged with doubt. It's unfair and wrong; she's a catch. As she tries on trousers longer than some people, I want to ask her whether she thinks there might be someone nice there this evening and that perhaps she might find love. As I start to broach the issue I am interrupted. One of Ellen's friends, Fran, who looks like the man-hungry, orange one from *The Golden Girls* says, 'Hey Ellen, Jim's here.' Who's Jim? Jim is a man in his fifties, slimish, with thinning grey hair, a well-preened goatee and the kind of uneven, blotchy skin that suggests he's the first to arrive at a party and the last to leave. With him is a very short lady in her twenties, checkout-girl attractive, with long brown hair. I introduce myself to her. She is called Britney. I didn't know that anybody except Britney Spears was actually called Britney. It will take some getting used to.

'And are you here for the weekend as well?' I ask.

'Yes I am, I work in the tall business,' she replies, in a sunny American accent.

'Do you? The tall business?'

'Yes, Ellen is actually one of our models,' she replies.

Wait. Slow down. I'm taking this in.

'Did you say you're in the tall business? What do you guys do?' I ask.

Jim leaps in to explain. Wearing a bright pink Oxford shirt and gold chain, there is the implication of raciness about this man. He's a 'sexy guy'.

'We do video websites with tall people, focussing on tall people. And Ellen is our newest model as a matter of fact, we just worked in Hawaii, doing filming,' he explains.

This is a big surprise. She's a dark horse, this Ellen. Still waters and all that ...

Jim takes out a professional-looking camera and begins snapping Ellen in various poses. Ellen is far from enthusiastic, but she seems to know what she is supposed to be doing, which appears to be to smile coyly and be very tall. Surprisingly, Britney (not Britney Spears – just someone also called Britney – I know, it's amazing) jumps in and poses alongside

her. Given that Britney is around five foot, this is clearly designed to illustrate Ellen's extraordinary height. They pose together for the shots, which are not without homoerotic undertones, while Britney plays with the absurdly long sleeves of one of the tall ladies' tops.

'And so, Jim, what's happening here?' I ask. Jim is snapping away, his Rolex slipping up and down his tanned, freckled wrist as he goes.

'What we wanted to show was a tall model next to a short person.'

'So Britney, you're the control on the experiment, is that right?' I ask.

'Something like that, yes. And just trying to take over having her show me all of the long pants compared to someone of a normal height,' he explains.

'So Jim, where are these photos going to end up?' I ask.

'These are going to end up on Ellen's website and within this we have different areas of the website. This will be called comparison.'

I have a good vibe from Jim, and decide to brave slightly choppier waters.

'So how do you feel about the sort of freakshow elements of this, you know, comparing the size of the hands? It's a bit like a Victorian freakshow isn't it?'

'I wouldn't use the word freak but I would use the word more as an object rather than a person.'

'Now Jim, you and I, we're men of the world,' the irony evaporates as the words leave my mouth. 'It's got to be that a lot of the men who subscribe to this website have a, you know, slight sexual thing going on?'

'You're right,' he says. 'Now here we go. Good Ellen, very nice. Very cute there. We are a small fetish and that's really the word for it. And obviously as with any fetish, there's a sexual element to it. Or it wouldn't be a fetish. But we don't carry that on any further than the shots that we do.'

Jim is very matter of fact about this, and I trust that he's telling the truth that the shoots don't get any more salacious than this. I don't feel we have another Woody here.

I go on, in my mild interrogation. 'So, what do you think Ellen thinks about that element of it? The fetish side.'

'Ellen is a schoolteacher, she's quite conservative and my guess would be maybe you just blot it out of your mind. It's an extra income, it's easy money, but nevertheless the important thing is her psyche. You know it's something that she's proud of.'

The brief photoshoot comes to an end. In spite of trying on a few items, Ellen passes on making a purchase. I don't blame her. One of the great bugbears of the tall females I've been mingling with is the difficulty in dressing stylishly. If this shop is anything to go by, I can understand why. As with shops I've been to that cater for tall men, there seems to be an assumption that if you are tall, you must be massively fat as well. There is a plain, shapeless, drab quality to the various items on sale. They might fit, but they don't look any good. I'm no Jeff Banks, but these clothes are essentially grannies' clothes. Which sends a depressing message to a young woman wanting to turn heads for something other than her height.

We leave the fusty-aired shop and its stench of viscose in extra large, to head back to the convention centre. Ellen gives me a lift in her man's car – a black Chevrolet Silverado.

Once we hit the freeway, Ellen puts this unrefined machine through its paces. She is a fast driver and claims you can do at least eighty without getting pulled over. She says this with the bravado of a London minicab driver unburdened with either a licence or insurance. Perhaps her phlegmatic attitude comes from the knowledge that whatever speed she does, she'll tower over any traffic officer who has the temerity to apprehend her.

I want to spoil the speed party by asking more about the fetishistic aspect of her modelling. It just doesn't seem to be a natural fit. Either she is unaware, or she's turning a blind eye. Or both. But of all the girls in the world to be appealing to men in macs, on their Macs, the least likely candidate is Ellen. As Jim mentioned, she is a homespun gal, a school-teacher without a salacious or exhibitionist bone in her body – and that's a lot of bone.

'So Ellen, do you put it to the back of your mind that there might be a fetish element to it?' I ask.

'No, I know there is because a lot of guys like they want to see me in the big six-inch heels. And I don't wear heels. I mean I just have real sensitive feet so ...'

Sensitive feet! This woman just wasn't born to titillate. I'm mystified as to why she does this. As I prepare to pursue this issue, my heart skips a beat as we take an unexpected, sharp turn off the freeway. As we come out of the bend, the steering wheel slides back swiftly through her massive hands, the kind of hands that could probably keep a German penalty ball out of England's net in a World Cup semi final.

Now that we are on another straight road and I'm slightly more confident I'm not going to die, I go on, 'How about bikinis and stuff, Ellen, will you do that?'

'Yes I do have some bikini shots. But they are conservative. I know that all my pictures are really conservative and I don't do anything that I am ashamed of or embarrassed about.' This I don't doubt. I'm beginning to suspect it is economic pragmatism that guides this whole endeavour. Topping up her teacher's salary with the occasional innocuous photoshoot, the contents over which she has full control might be a bit of a no-brainer. But there's something deeply moral about Ellen, and it still surprises that me that she can reconcile innocent shots of her in a trouser suit, or ball gown being enjoyed by a man in another part of the country, with his trousers around his ankles. Perhaps the attention – not that kind, but the positive stuff – is a bit of an ego boost.

'Are you flattered, in some ways, by this attention?'

'Yes, I am. I actually get a few emails from guys asking me to marry them.'

A visit later to Jim's surprisingly chaotic and messy hotel room confirmed two things. Firstly Britney is more than just a bag carrier and 'model'. Either that or she sleeps on the floor. And secondly, Jim's online empire isn't family viewing. To describe the tame shots of Ellen in various smart, sensible outfits across a variety of mundane locations as the thin edge of the wedge would be an understatement.

Jim explains, 'We have Bunny Glamours. She's more an exotic model.'

Bunny Glamours (I'm guessing that's her stage name) is built like a New Zealand rugby player. Massively tall, broad, muscular and, inevitably, large-chested. The shots, some topless, some bottomless, feature a small man she appears to be verbally abusing and generally dominating.

'Then you have your foot area, then your fetish heels area. And boxing.' Oh Jesus. I've seen enough. I'm only just getting over Woody, and the 'nasty stuff'.

In fact Jim has eleven tall women on his roster, and to be fair, though the vast majority of them are essentially pornographic shots, the Ellen section could make the web surfer think he's accidentally clicked on the Kay's catalogue autumn

collection. But it's still curious that Ellen is willing to be in the same ball park, sharing the same stage as these other 'ladies'. I guess money talks, and the Silverado doesn't buy its own brake pads or pay for its own tyres. And I'd say the money's decent. Jim tells me the website itself gets hundreds of thousands of hits and he turned over a million dollars last year in subscriptions and DVD sales. Perhaps too, for Ellen, after a lifetime of being the physical oddball, and somewhat unlucky in love, it's gratifying to know there are a bunch of guys out there, not necessarily all pervs, who just think the way she looks is beautiful, and perhaps sexy. How bad can that be? And I think that's the conclusion this level-headed and insanely likeable woman has come to. And frankly, fair enough.

I leave Jim's hotel room – the Hugh Hefner of tall women – and return to my hotel bedroom for a shower, a shave and half an hour of *Murder She Wrote*. You don't have to concentrate – all 83,750 episodes just blend into each other. It must be a later one, because the camera work does that weird thing in which the picture is crystal clear for all the other characters and strangely misty for shots of Angela Lansbury. No doubt Vaseline on the close-up lens was specified in our Ange's hefty contract negotions. But in this episode, the frosting of the lens has reached the point at which Jessica Fletcher appears to be trapped in an almost Dickensian fog, her face, just a supernatural blur, her nodding, henlike head barely recognisable. I doze through the reveal at the end. I think it was the fairground owner that did it. Oh no, that's Scooby Doo.

I look at my watch and it's 5.30 p.m. Incredibly I'm late! The big party has started and I'm late. They actually eat dinner at 5.30. I've had to get used to this strange aspect of the American culture. Outside of metropolitan centres like New York and LA, people generally eat very early. Many restaurants in the USA close at 8.30 p.m. or 9, which is about when we start getting peckish in 'Old Europe'. I have come unstuck many a time thanks to this and had to see just how I can trick my body into thinking a Dunkin Donuts is dinner. Luckily, sort of, places like Jenny's and McDonalds are open around the clock. But I think I'd rather have a donut.

Tonight I am not intending any such high jinks, and am struck by the warmth in the room. It is a communion, a coming together. A little bubble of tolerance, appreciation and understanding, in cowboy boots. I'm informed during the meal, by a couple who have been doing this pilgrimage annually for two decades, that the society started as a dating event for lovelorn lankies. Touchingly, this couple, now in their late fifties, actually met at this event, all those years ago. And there are many others here tonight who also wouldn't be together if it wasn't for the tall club. As the group take the short stroll from dining area to dance hall, and the faux

electronic beat of early Eighties pop music, I am genuinely moved by the tenderness on show here. There is actually real vulnerability in being exceedingly tall, and all I can think now, is what a brave and strong bunch they are. As Ellie and others told me, it's one weekend in the year that they can really look forward to. A time to completely relax and not be remotely self-conscious, and even rejoice in what is in many ways a gift. And once the weekend's over, they pack up their big hats and sequinned waistcoats; it's back to 363 days of being mildly stared at. I came away liking tall people, and feeling a bit sorry for them. I'm still not sure whether I'm one of them.

Before I dive off to my room and enjoy a quick hit of *Diagnosis Murder*, I join a number of the women on the dance floor for a particularly energetic boogie to Michael Jackson's 'Bad' – *shamoa!* It's an out-of-body experience for me to dance with a woman taller than me. As we then dance badly to something by the Rolling Stones, I ask Ellie if anyone has caught her eye tonight.

'No,' she replies swiftly.

'OK ... Not even potential, somebody you could change maybe, improve a bit?' I ask.

'No!' she retorts. She goes on to explain the issue at play when it comes to the unfairer sex.

'A lot of guys are like six foot four and are intimidated by me. And then guys that are six foot two and under are like a

lot shorter, you know, aren't interested. And I'm not always comfortable with someone, like, under six two.'

'But you're always kind of trying slightly?'

'I'm always looking, yeah.'

I'm going to miss Ellen and I hope she gets the man she deserves. I think she will. And I just hope he isn't one of her online fans.

I am aware Ellen is the thin edge of the wedge when it comes to tall women. All these tall females are in someone's shadow – that of Sandy Allen. An American, in her fifties, who is claimed to be the tallest woman in the world. I ask Ellen about her.

'So, do you know Sandy Allen?'

'Yes, sure.'

'OK and who exactly is she?'

'She's the tallest woman in the world, in the US I think anyway.'

'And do you have any idea how tall she actually is?'

'Seven foot seven,' she replies.

'Seven foot seven? Give me some perspective, how high would that be?'

'Well my reach is what, nine foot five. I don't know, she's probably let's see, right here, but I haven't seen her stand up.' She raises her hand close to the ceiling. It would appear Sandy Allen is as tall as a room. It's good to hear that Sandy's astonishing height isn't apocryphal and I'm already excited

at the prospect of meeting her. Encountering Ellen and her tall buddies has been a great way of entering this world.

'Listen, Ellen, I just want to say what a joy it's been to meet you.'

'Do you want another tall hug before you go?' she asks. I'm thrilled at this warm and symbolic offer. I've now done one of the *things to do before you die,* twice! It's been really great meeting Ellen and entering this oasis of lankiness. This is a club I never knew I was a member of, but Ellen's kind offer of a hug tells me I'm firmly in it. What's exciting about this weekend is that it hasn't just brought me up to speed with some of the issues around extreme female height; it's presented me with a lead that could take me to the upper echelons of how tall a woman can physically be. As I wander back to my room, I muse on my time with Ellen. There's nothing that different about her to any other single young woman about town. It's curious therefore, that her height has reached the tipping point of common 'acceptability'. A few inches shorter, and she's an Amazonian goddess. Instead, her height has tipped her into the realms of being an online oddity, that a select group of men will pay good money to gawp at. She deserves better.

As I flick the many TV channels on offer from my bed, in denial of the brutally early flight that awaits me in the morning, I'm curious as to how life might be for someone like Sandy Allen, who quite literally towers over the likes of Ellen. What can someone like that really look like in the flesh? What are the practicalities of life for a woman not far off eight feet in height? Does she have a job, a husband, a home? Is it fun, or a curse? Put frankly, what's it *like*? Well, there's only one way to find out ...

* * *

Ever my mother's son, I decide to ring ahead to the tallest woman in the world, to warn her of my impending arrival. The sun has returned to Arizona with a vengeance. I'm standing in the desert, between my hotel and the airport, leaning against my Ford Expedition, my lower back being gently toasted by the heat of the fender. The air is so hot and dry it slightly scorches my throat with every breath. I can feel my skin tanning in literally seconds. There is air con in the car and *The Eagles Greatest Hits* cued up in the CD player, so I'll try to keep this brief. The phone rings. I'm getting a bit giddy. This is one of a handful of the world's most extraordinary people. And I'm about to have a chat with her on the phone. But my excitement is curtailed. I hear the brutal click of the answering machine.

'Hi, you've reached the home of the Jolly Green Giant. Thanks for calling. Leave a message after the tone. Beep.'

It is the voice of a man. A man with a deep voice. The kind of man who would make the ice road truckers look like girlies. I'm forced to assume, though, that it is not a man. It must be Sandy Allen, and having a deep voice must be another of the symptoms of being that big.

'Hi this is a message for the Jolly Green Giant, aka Sandy,' I play along with the green giant conceit – Sandy may be very fond of that gag. 'It's Mark Dolan here from England. I was given your number by some of the guys at the Tall Club of Arizona; I hope that's OK. I'd love to come and see you. I'm arriving this evening in Indianapolis and would love to try to come and see you some time tomorrow if that's possible. I hope you are well and look forward to catching up with you soon. Many thanks.'

Now my voice is sitting on the voicemail of the World's Tallest Woman. Another first. I drive up to Phoenix Airport, leaving the car at the purpose-built car hire building, which is like an airport in itself and which is located what feels like 150 miles from the airport itself. It's an adjustment going from a climate-controlled, leather-clad SUV, to rattling around inside a vast empty bus not engineered for turning. But I'll live.

After quite the most laborious transition through Phoenix Airport security, during which I was prodded and examined so thoroughly, I've effectively had an affair, I get onto the plane and begin my journey one and a half thousand miles east, to meet Sandy. Fifty-two-year-old Sandy has held her title since she was nineteen. It has given her the colourful life of a celebrity. She's made numerous television appearances across the world, met film stars and appeared in an Oscar-winning Fellini movie. The movie was *Casanova*, a 1976 picture, in which she played Wondrous Angelina, the Giantess. As definitive a case of typecasting as you'll ever find. She was clearly no stranger to self-promotion. Someone had even named a song after her, a dittie named 'Hello Sandy Allen' by the band Split Enz and written by Neil Fin. I'm suitably impressed.

As I arrive at Indianapolis Airport and shiver as an icy wind pierces through my coat and stabs my warm skin, I'm struck by how it can be arctic in one part of a country and boiling hot desert in another. The other spooky phenomenon to get used to as a Brit is flying from a US airport, and after seven hours in the air, still being in America. This never fails to impress me.

It's actually snowing in Indianapolis, and the drive to Sandy's place on the outskirts of Indiana's biggest city doesn't throw up any great visual treats. As I drive past malls, drive-thrus and timber-clad residential neighbourhoods, it just feels like more of the same. More Stars and Stripes flags, more picket fences, more branches of Sizzler and Wendy Burger and Red Robin; more Starbucks, more JC Penny, more Days Inn, more America. And frankly, it's all a bit joyless and lonely.

I'm close to Shelbyville, Sandy's home for all her fifty-two years. The snow and the bleak emptiness of the surrounding fields lend it a certain drama and romance. But essentially there's nothing really here. Five years ago, Sandy moved into residential care, unable to cater for her own considerable physical needs. Lugging a 7 ft 7 in frame around into your mid forties is bound to take its toll. Unfortunately, I am to learn that Sandy's health takes a lot of twists and turns, and I am saddened to hear that as I arrive, she has had to temporarily leave her care home and go into hospital. As I make my way there, I decide to pop in, meet the people who look after her and find out just how poorly she is.

I arrive at the home, which is a modern, single-storeyed medical facility in the middle of the frosted countryside. It certainly feels more like a hospital than a home, but the atmosphere is convivial and professional. And it doesn't smell. I wander corridor after corridor, wondering whether there is an official reception area. As I flit past open doors, I see white head after white head, in various states of decrepitude. I'm struck by how premature it must feel to have wound up here at the age of forty-seven. That is the age at which a woman is at full speed as a human being – armed with knowledge, wisdom, strength, a knowing cynicism combined with a willingness to be surprised. And for all its fastidious hygiene and ebulliently friendly atmosphere, it's not really what you want at forty-seven.

I'm looking for Nadine – she's in charge. I've been wandering corridors for a good four or five minutes. I've walked past bathrooms, boiler rooms, bedrooms, supplies rooms, kitchens, but in all my wanderings I haven't seen anyone with a badge and a face that says 'can I help you?' As I encounter yet more corridors, I feel like I've wandered onto the set of *The Shining*. I'm expecting Jack Nicholson at any point to hack his axe through one of the doors and exclaim 'Here's Johnny!' Spared a grizzly, Stephen King-inspired fate, I take a lucky turn and am greeted with the oasis-like sight of a hub of nurses, milling around their photocopiers and fax machines.

I spot who I think must be Nadine. A glamorous woman, shortish, with dark black, wavy hair and plenty of slap on her forty-something face. She has a managerial air, with clipboard in hand and I have the immediate and completely unfounded impression that she is outstandingly good at her job. As we begin to talk, she seems to have that near-perfect balance required of anyone in charge of anything. It's a balance of wry good humour, combined with a firm professionalism. I resume my tour of the Kubrick corridors, but this time alongside someone who knows where the hell we are going.

After exchanging pleasantries, we come to the pressing matter of Sandy's health. I had no idea she was remotely poorly, so I wasn't expecting to be broaching this issue as part of my journey. My feeling when anybody is ill is to back right off. Unfortunately when you've travelled thousands of miles and have a finite amount of time in a given location, and with a United Airlines ticket that will have you hung, drawn and quartered if you try to change it, I have little option than for Sandy not being well to be part of the story. Or the whole story. It depends just how serious her illness is. I ask Nadine if she is gravely ill.

'No, she's actually much better,' she says, hair bouncing as we stride along the corridor. How can she, half my height, be walking more quickly than me? But she is.

'So what was up with Sandy?' I ask in an unnecessarily American vernacular. I've been here a week or two – surely it's rather too soon to develop a transatlantic drawl.

'Her body, as tall as it is, had an infection and that's a lot of infection when you're that tall,' she explains.

Nadine has offered me a tour of the place. I don't really need one, but it would be churlish to decline the offer. It's like the head chef of a restaurant offering you a tour of the kitchen. I don't really need to – I know what a cooker looks like, but it's an unspoken rule that you don't say no.

'Did you want to see the shower room first?' says Nadine. This is too detailed a tour now. I've flown all the way here to meet the tallest woman in the world, and I'm checking out shower heads.

'Oh yes that would be great, please, thank you,' I say. 'Do you think Sandy would mind me seeing all this?' I ask, as it dawns on me this is most probably the shower room Sandy herself uses.

'No I don't think she would care. She hangs out here. Takes about an hour and a half to do her shower.' That figures.

Nadine authoritatively opens the door of the shower room.

'Hello?' comes a little, frail, damp voice from inside the shower room.

Nadine, with reflexes like a salamander, swings the door shut again.

'OK never mind!' she says, with a wry smile on her face. 'Well, we can't do that.'

After this bruising incident, Nadine takes me straight to Sandy's room. I'm given a clue as to how extraordinary Sandy is by looking at her bed, which is, of course long and fairly wide. But it's also fantastically high. It's like the story of the princess and the pea, after the twenty mattresses have been piled on top of each other. Nadine explains that this tall princess needs the height so she can slide out of a morning, on to her wheelchair.

The mental picture I have of Sandy is standing and smiling. That's what you do when you are supernaturally tall – smile a lot. Or so it seems from my many internet sorties into this world. If you are born unique, you are not allowed to look anything other than utterly jolly, and delighted to be so different. There is no room in our collective psyche for physically unique people to be anything but beaming from ear to ear at their predicament. It's a barrel of laughs, being the biggest or smallest, thinnest or fattest – or at least that's the expectation we have as a public, for a bunch of uniquely vulnerable people who in fact need, more than most, to drop the smile and be supported and protected. It fits with that cliché we have of fat people laughing and smiling and being jolly 24/7. That's not because they are. It's pressure to be so, and a defence mechanism against being judged, or worse, felt sorry for. But I suspect it's also a barrier to change and thus ultimately self-destructive. If the message being sent out is 'hey I'm fine, great in fact, don't worry about me', then this inevitably perpetuates the status quo.

'Goodness gracious, goes right up to there. That's a big old bed,' I say.

'And those are Sandy's shoes', explains Nadine. 'And her club got together and donated money and had those special made for Sandy,' she says, presenting me with what appear to be a supersized equivalent of the kind of humble and utilitarian black shoes worn by nuns. And they don't look remotely comfortable.

In spite of one or two objects that give a clue to Sandy's height, it's amazing just how homogenising of the personality these institutions can be. The room, though comfortable, clean and warm, is just like the tens of others, and there's little evidence it's home to the tallest woman in the world. If you are female and 7 ft 7 in and you still don't stand out as an individual, there's really no hope for the armies of white-haired pensioners hoping to catch this nurse's or that nurse's eye.

There are a number of what appear to be gifts littered around the room, including greetings cards and a number of soft toys.

'So, just how reliant is Sandy on other people's generosity?' I ask Nadine.

'Oh very reliant, because of the lack of funds. She only gets 52 dollars a month from the state.'

I am shocked at this figure. So America doesn't think she's worthy of note either. 'So where would she be without other people's handouts and gifts?' I ask.

'Probably without,' she replies, frankly.

I explore the issue of Sandy's position and try to glean how much a big deal it is to have her in this home, if at all.

'So Sandy, she's something of a star here really, isn't she?' I ask.

'She is a star here but we also have another celebrity.'

Now the term 'celebrity' is experiencing a bit of mental fatigue these days, so I'm not holding my breath.

'Oh,' I ask. 'And who is that?'

'We also have the oldest lady in the world,' she replies proudly.

'Really?'

'Absolutely.' Nadine is one of those people who says 'absolutely', when she means 'absolutely'.

'You've got the oldest lady in the world?' I am genuinely taken aback.

'You bet,' she replies, her neck craned up to talk to me. 'Famous building,' she goes on, in that upbeat American way that is celebratory of everything. 'Famous building,' she repeats, in case I missed it first time.

'So you have the oldest lady. And the tallest one!'

'And the tallest, that's right.'

'How did that happen?' I ask.

'Lucky little town.'

A fantastic answer. I'm slightly in awe of this woman.

'Would you like to go meet Miss Edna?'

'I would love to go and meet Miss Edna.'

'She's 114 years old, so be gentle,' Nadine warns me wryly.

'Oh my goodness. Do you have any tips for me about how to sort of talk to her?' I'm in a flap.

'Very loudly in her ear, because she can't hear very well,' replies Nadine factually.

'Great, I can't believe it. Is she really the tallest woman in the world?'

'No,' she replies swiftly.

'Sorry, my brain is frazzled.' I'm in an utter tailspin. I might need a sedative and a lie down. And I'm in the perfect place.

We head towards Miss Edna's room. Ah, Miss Edna – she's already a legend being called that. That's enough for me. She had me at Miss Edna.

'Is there some pressure on your part to keep her alive?' I ask Nadine.

'Oh yeah. You bet. Don't want anything happening to her on my watch.'

A characteristically sensational answer from Nadine. I love that she uses the term 'my watch'. She talks like a prison guard in a Stephen King novella. If I asked her British equivalent the same question about pressure to keep an elderly resident alive, I'd receive a soul-shredding spiel about health and safety and the perennial threat of death. Here in the snows of Shelbyville, it's all a lot more matter of fact. 'She ain't gonna do no dyin' on my watch!' God, I might have to end my days here, under Nadine's watchful eye and unforgiving sponge.

We walk into Miss Edna's room. Her grandson is there – himself a properly middle-aged, I've-lived-a-life, man in his fifties. And there she is. All 114 years of her. She is tiny, sitting neatly on a massive armchair. Though 114, she looks no more than ninety. A compliment I'll resist making.

'Hello, Miss Edna, my name's Mark; it's lovely to meet you.' At this point I'm yelling, as instructed by Nadine. I extend my hand. Nothing happens. She just looks at my hand like it's a strange foreign object, unclear what I'm intending to do with it. Many seconds pass. It's high comedy, but I'm not laughing. It's too uncomfortable. As I prepare to seize the initiative by actually taking her hand into mine, her grandson steps in to help.

'He'd like to shake your hand,' he says, less loudly than me, but clearly more effectively.

'Oh,' she says, in a soft, light, weathered voice.

Edna takes her suspicious eyes off my hand and takes it into hers, warmly.

'May I kiss your hand?' I ask, suddenly confident.

Miss Edna smiles and nods softly. If you can nod softly. Which she can.

I kiss her small, bony hand. Her pale, freckled skin is loosely wrapped around her fingers, like a knuckleduster wrapped in a tortilla.

'You're the oldest lady in the world. Are you proud that you're so special?' I ask, again at maximum decibels, so that even the freezing sheep outside can hear me.

'I suppose so. I don't know ...' Her eyes dart around for an answer she doesn't have. She is beautiful; her hair, Ariel Automatic white, her skin dappled with freckles and a touch of rouge. I've seen people half her age in poorer nick. There isn't the slightest hint she is about to cease to hold her record.

'What's your secret to a long life?' I ask predictably. But I do want to know.

'I don't know, I don't think I have one,' she says. It's like she hasn't really countenanced such a question before. It seems her answer is tailing off until she pipes up again by saying, 'Just healthy, I guess.' That'll teach me to be profound. I have my answer to longevity and it's the boring, but correct

answer. The answer the majority of us are running away from, as we tuck into that Yorkie bar.

From various sets of eyes exchanging glances around the room, it's clearly time for me to wrap this one up. I certainly don't want to tire Miss Edna, or in any way hasten her demise. Not on Nadine's watch, anyway.

'Miss Edna, it's been a privilege to meet you,' I say. It has been.

'And you,' she replies sweetly.

She smells of warm milk and biscuits, as anyone over ninety should, and she has an aura that emits calm and comfort. One hundred and fourteen or not, she's a special, dignified person and having met a number of people on my travels who have ridden roughshod over the best interests of their own bodies, she is an inspiration. I suspect her long life comes not only from being 'just healthy'. Miss Edna seems to be at peace with herself, and the world.

As I get up to leave I say 'Thank you', thinking that my audience with this particular queen is over.

Miss Edna looks up, smiling. 'Maybe I'll see you again?' she says.

'I hope so,' I reply enthusiastically, though less sure inside, not being a gambling man.

'Yes me too ...' she says again. I'm amazed she's warmed to me in spite of my inane questions. It's a tender and unexpected diversion on my journey that I won't forget.

Nadine is hovering. She gives me the 'wrap this up' sign and ushers me firmly out of Miss Edna's room, like an overzealous PR person at a Tom Cruise junket. I've had my four minutes with the star, time's up. And the star I'm really looking for is Sandy Allen. Actually, Sandy must be a star, because she has 'people'. And they are waiting in Nadine's office.

On the way, I'm still musing over my wonderful and spontaneous visit with Miss Edna. And about a year later, on 26 November 2008, I realised how special that encounter was. It was the day I was queuing up at a Starbucks in London and, through boredom, was flicking through the news on my phone. Miss Edna's soft, smiling face popped up, next to a story about her sad death from natural causes at the age of 115. She left five grandchildren, thirteen great-grandchildren and thirteen great-great grandchildren. They will miss her and treasure her memory, and so will I.

* * *

Nadine's office is the same size and shape as Sandy's bedroom. In fact the same as every room on the complex. It's an egalitarian piece of architecture, to say the least. Sandy's 'people' are her dearest, oldest and it turns out, only friends. They are called Jane and Linda. Conveniently Jane and Linda are the same height as each other. In fact, they look like sisters, with perhaps a ten-year age gap. Jane is bespectacled, with dyed red hair and has the width to go with her lack of height. Similarly Linda is short and stout, but with greying hair and a pale complexion. It's as though the 7 ft 7 in Sandy Allen chose friends who were the mirror opposite of herself. She chose well, because together, unfunded, they run her life. As well as ferrying her not inconsiderable frame around, they deliver all the basic sundry items she needs in her life, including books, music, sweets, clothes, footwear.

They even stump up for the repair and maintenance of her Sandymobile, an extraordinary, purpose-built van specially customised for Sandy's height. Large and blue, with a massively high roof to accommodate Sandy in her wheelchair, it resembles a supersized popemobile. We step out of the warm care home and climb into the Sandywagon. In classic American understatement, Sandy's name is daubed all over the van, in massive lettering, proudly declaring her to be 'Sandy Allen – Tallest Woman In The World – 7 ft 7 ins!!' The van was a gift from well-wishers. Even an ageing and vulnerable celebrity like Sandy is subject to the unforgiving nature of the American economy. These two tiny and unremittingly caring women, who are of limited means themselves, are keeping Sandy going, morally and financially. And it feels like a scandal.

Jane is driving the three of us in the Sandyvan, as we head to the hospital to see the woman whose name is on the

vehicle. On the way to hospital, amid another icy flurry, the sky bleach-white with snow, we make a pitstop at Sandy's favourite eaterie, Grandma's Pancake House, on South Harrison Street in Shelbyville, the kind of eaterie, which, if I had been Elvis, I would have travelled hundreds of miles to have a snack at. Great vast breakfasts, burgers, pitchers of Coke, pancakes the size of tabletops and as much cholesterol-rich cheesecake as you can shake a jar of betablockers at. Even by US standards, the portions are big, which is no doubt one of the big selling points for Our Sand. Jane makes the order. The smiley waitress gets scribbling, like a swot in a school exam.

'OK, she needs turkey, mashed potatoes, lots of gravy, fried mushrooms ... and give her that chocolate and green cake that she likes so much,' commands Jane.

'So how many people have you just ordered for there really?' I ask.

'Two,' she replies.

'Right, so you have to order double portions for her?' I say.

'Yes and she won't share her cake with you; I'm going to guarantee it,' adds Linda with a smirk.

We leave 'Grandma's', which is a similar experience to being a character leaving the room in an episode of *Happy Days*, as our departure is greeted with myriad cheers and 'goodbye y'all's'. Back in the Sandymachine I touch on the importance of the title of 'tallest woman in the world' to her. Her friends are in no doubt.

'It's very important to her; it's all she has now,' Jane explains. Apparently this isn't her only record. 'Now she supposedly is the world's oldest living giant in recorded history because the only one we can find older than her was Goliath in the Bible.' Now *that's* a statistic.

Preparing myself for this encounter with the great lady, I say: 'Ladies, do you have any advice for me about how to be around Sandy?'

'Give her a kiss,' Linda says. She then smiles and says, 'Check your hands with her first and just see the difference. She's quite a handful, big handful.' They both laugh. I don't think I'll need to compare my hand with hers to get a sense of how big she is. I think the 7 ft 7 in of height will do that for me.

As we go into the hospital, I'm actually quite nervous about meeting this giant woman. I don't know why, but for some reason if I was meeting a giant man I could manage those emotions but I just don't know what to expect from a massively tall female. If I am to be honest, it's probably because being a massively tall female is a bit freaky. Something primal - and bloody stupid - in me, suggests I am about to meet a monster. I am ashamed about having these irrational anxieties and I'm hoping they'll evaporate once I properly meet Sandy. I suppose, also, that anyone that big is physically intimidating; that's sort of what nature has, rightly or wrongly, programmed into us.

The girls guide me to what seems to be Sandy's room. There is a deep voice emanating from it. It's the same voice as the voice in the 'jolly green giant' recorded message.

'Sandy? Is that you?'

I walk into the room, and there, in all her supersized glory, is Sandy. That she is lying down in the bed, covered in sheets hides an immediate sense of her scale. In fact the first thing I notice, as the girls warned me, are her hands. They are the size of tennis rackets. And her huge, massive face. A long, wide, almost Neanderthal face that, if it weren't for the rouge on her cheeks and the red emulsion on her lips, would surely belong to a very manly man. The kind of man who could have assembled Stonehenge by himself, in one busy afternoon.

'Hi Sandy. My name is Mark Dolan and it's an absolute joy to meet you.' I walk towards her bed, and following the diplomatic advice given to me earlier, I say, 'May I kiss you?'

'If you would like to kiss me,' she says coquettishly. The tallest woman in the world is being coquettish with me! I climb up the bed to reach her large face. I peck her on the cheek, and it's like kissing the side of a craggy mountain. Her skin itself, though, is incredibly soft, like that of a freshly plucked rabbit. And there is a feminine scent coming from the dusting of make-up on her face which contradicts the truck-driver features.

'And the other side, this is the European way,' I say.

'Oh, I see,' she says diplomatically.

I use the full length of my body to reach the other side. Why am I making life so hard for myself? To achieve this feat of kissing her on both cheeks, at least one of my feet is off the floor and I am effectively resting my chest on top of hers, horizontally, in the bed. I have all but climbed into bed with the tallest woman in the world. A woman who is in hospital, ill. She is wearing a satin nightie and it's suddenly, unintentionally, all far too intimate. What's wrong with a warm shake of the hand?

'Two cheeks, there you go,' I say, bringing to an end my insane kissing palaver. 'It's lovely to meet you', I add. 'And this, by the way, is a bit of lunch.' I produce the goods from 'Grandma's'.

'Oh my goodness!' she booms briefly, before quickly adding, 'If you want to sit it over there.' Her faux surprise is short lived as is the case with anyone who is used to being something of a queen, receiving guests and gifts and the like. With this delivery of food, I feel like one of Luciano Pavarotti's minions must have felt, having perhaps run for miles to bring him a bowl of his prized spag bol, only to be told by the great man, 'Stick it in the microwave, I'll be down in five.'

Standing a safe and less compromising distance from a woman I've effectively mauled, we can begin a normal conversation.

'You OK?' she asks.

Her voice is possibly the most remarkable thing about Sandy. Yes, the well-quoted statistic of her height is no doubt accurate. But I'm particularly struck by her voice. It is a deep, booming, man's voice. Her bass notes reverberate throughout the room, bouncing off all the hard surfaces before spooling together and heading out the door and down the corridor. Her voice literally travels. At this moment I'm struck by who she's been reminding me of. With the deep voice, the large, primal face and huge smile packed with many teeth – she's Jaws. Not the shark. The character from James Bond from the Roger Moore era (Moore easily being my favourite Bond, by the way – I'm not a snob about these things). Jaws was a menacing giant who, apart from being built like a brick shithouse, had a set of metal teeth that he could use to chew through metal cable. There's nothing menacing about Sandy, but her extraordinary body and voice do remind me of the actor Richard Kiel who played the aforementioned Bond villain. Ironically, Richard Kiel is titchy compared to Sandy, as he stands at under 7 foot 2 inches, five inches short of the lady.

'I'm very well, Sandy,' I respond. 'It's just fantastic to meet you. And I'd love to touch on how you got to be such a tall lady; can I ask you a bit about that?'

'Certainly,' she begins. 'When I was born I was an average-size baby. I weighed 7 pounds 14 ounces and I was 21 inches long. But my grandmother tells me by the time I reached the

age of ten I was already about six foot three, six foot five inches tall.

'You were six foot five at the age of?' I ask, making sure I'm not hearing things.

'Ten,' she replies definitely.

'I'm six foot four and a half inches,' I say with an authority bestowed upon me by the gang at the Tall Club in Arizona – bless their socks. 'And so you were taller than I am at the age of ten?'

'Yes. A little bit.'

'Wow ...' And wow is right – it's astonishing. The image of a ten year old being taller than me now, and a female ten year old at that, is the definition of extraordinary. I'm picturing this ten-year-old girl wandering around sleepy, small-town Shelbyville in the early 1970s, standing at nearly two metres in height. People must have been blessing themselves and looking up at the sky. She is amazing to behold now, but the idea of a little girl being a physical giant is even more shocking, because of the unworldly contrast between her body and her age. It's mother nature getting her sums very badly wrong.

'So, what role did your grandmother have in your life?' I ask, having been given a steer by Linda on the way in the car that she was pretty much Sandy's main carer.

'She is the one that raised me; my mother didn't want to bring me up. My grandmother was a big influence in my life.

She is the one that taught me not to pay attention to other people when they were trying to be cruel.'

She pauses, her pretty blue eyes peering and blinking through her metal-framed glasses. Her eyes, the only part of her not supernaturally large. Just normal, if I dare use the word.

'Were people cruel to you, Sandy?' I ask, trying to be gentle with this giant.

'Yes, I did go through some tough times with the kids at school, especially the boys,' she says. 'I didn't get to participate in very many of the dances or anything because none of the boys wanted to take a girl that was two feet taller than he was.' Although a comical image, the sadness in Sandy's voice is genuinely moving. All these years later and she's understandably still hurting.

'And how much does it mean to you to have the title of the World's Tallest Woman?' I ask.

'Well, I'm very proud of my height,' she says.

'Is there no bitterness? I mean surely there must have been occasions when you thought "why me?"'

'Oh there were a few times when I wished I could have fallen in love with someone and gotten married and had a family and lived a "normal" life.' She goes on – she's in full flow. 'Oh I've met my fair share of shorter guys that have been nuts about tall women. In fact I even had a marriage proposal from someone who was the leader of a tribe in Nigeria.'

'Has there ever been a man who could have been the one?' I ask, addressing one of the two key concerns among the women I met in Arizona, the other being finding jeans that fit.

'Oh yes,' she says. 'There was ...' she lingers on this thought. 'But I'm a typical female. I'd like to rest on their shoulder and be protected by them. I wouldn't want to be the man in the family, so to speak.'

Inside this huge body, Sandy seems such a fragile soul. She clearly craves a loving relationship, something many take for granted. The trappings of fame, the visitors, the gifts, the personalised van – they are all scant compensation. Having met many people on my travels whose dysfunctional life is self-inflicted, it strikes me as so unfair that to be born as different as Sandy is pretty much guarantees she won't be able to get married and experience the things the rest of us feel we have a right to. Why Sandy? What has she done wrong to merit this life sentence in which experiencing love is a practical impossibility? Many choose the path of fame and set out on a mission to be noticed. Sandy chose no such fate, so to have notoriety foisted upon you from early childhood and be stripped of the basic human right of love is very sad.

Thus as I head out of the hospital, having given Sandy a far more common-or-garden kiss on departure (I'm learning), it occurs to me that she is more than a physical giant.

She is a giant person. Somehow her spirit seems to fill that vast body and soar out of it, touching the rest of us. I've only been in Sandy's company a day, but I've already been drawn in. My anxieties prior to meeting her have disappeared. I can see why Linda and Jane have slavishly tended to her over the years. They love her, and they are in awe of her. She's a Queen, wearing the crown of tallest woman in the world. But for how long? Both her fluctuating health and more immediately a possible rival in China may bring to an untimely end Sandy's reign.

I go back to my hotel, a low-rise, low-rent business hotel on the outskirts of town. The *business* bit of *business hotel* is rather spurious. It's like any other slightly cheap and nasty American hotel, except it's got wifi, and a printer at reception. Well hoo-bloody-ray. Bill Gates could stay here, and he'd be pinching himself at the sheer level of resource available to a man keen to do *business*. As night falls, and the cars on the motorway outside seem to get louder and faster, I turn in my bed, dreaming of Jaws and his shiny teeth. I wake horribly early, thanks to the sound of a fan heater that inexplicably kicks in at 5 a.m. Who gets suddenly chilly at 5 a.m.? Surely if you've survived the cold until 5 a.m., you'll hobble along for the last hour or two of your sleep. It's like America's entrance into the Second World War – a nice gesture, but a bit too late to be truly grateful for. I wander down the staircase to reception – something no-one does in this country – I've literally never seen it happen and I always get strange looks whenever I head *past* the lift, and into the stairwell.

I help myself to the free breakfast, wishing it wasn't free and simply a bit better. I neck a thin, weak coffee and scoff a bun that tastes like it was designed for astronauts. Actually it's a blessing in disguise, as I'll need to save myself for the inevitable pitstop at Grandma's Pancake House on the way to Sandy.

And so, after a half an hour at said establishment, I'm a new man. I have a tummy full of eggs, hash browns and pancakes, all washed down with good coffee and some very yellow orange juice. Now I'm ready for action; it's time to get the tallest woman in the world out of her hospital bed, into her van and home. As I arrive through the automatic sliding doors of the hospital, I say 'good morning' to a number of ill people on my way in; as is typical of this country I am greeted with winning smiles and a fulsome return of my good wishes. In America, even the sick people say 'Have a nice day'. Even if it's their last.

I greet Jane and Linda; they smile warmly but are jaded: they have Sandy fatigue. As we wait to be called upstairs to collect Sandy, I ask the girls about the issue of Sandy's health.

'Listen, why do you think she's wound up in hospital this time?' I ask.

'Because she's Sandy,' replies Jane, with a wry smile. Lynda laughs and says 'right'.

Jane goes on. 'She gets depressed, she doesn't eat, she won't take her medicine. She gets into a debilitated state and then by the time she decides to turn it around, it's too late and she ends up in the hospital for a few days.'

Lynda chips in. It's like a conversation between a long-married couple – it's them, and me. 'I mean she's going to be fifty-three. Do you think that people at fifty-three really want to be in a nursing home?' she asks validly.

'Have they been getting worse these depressions?' I ask.

'I'll be honest with you, every time we get a call saying they're going to take her to the hospital it's like OK is it this time? I'm sorry ...' Jane's face turns red and she begins to well up. She pushes her clenched fist to her lips, and a tear drops from her eye. To witness this level of affection and concern for Sandy is extremely touching. She is very lucky to have these two little women in her life. It's scary to think what might have become of this American national treasure if they weren't around.

We all regain our composure and I give them both a hug, before we head to the lift to pick up the patient.

As I enter the doorway of Sandy's room, I ask, 'So, where's the leggy blond?'

'Right here!" comes a cheery, deep voice from behind a crowd of nurses. They back away to reveal a smiling Sandy, resplendent in a shiny blue tracksuit and massive, gleaming white trainers. It turns out this entire outfit is one of many hand-me-down gifts from the 7 ft 1 in basketball player Shaquille O'Neal – what a guy!

As I push Sandy's unfeasible bulk in her special wheelchair towards the lift, she explains the precise medical nature of her condition. Her abnormal growth is nothing to do with having a tall gene. In fact, she had a tumour on her pituitary gland, diagnosed in her teens. The physical pressure on the gland, which produces growth hormone, caused her to grow and grow. And for the last few years, she's been wheelchair-bound, unable to take the strain of her enormous body. As we leave the hospital building and head out to the car park, my lower back is feeling the pressure of pushing her wheelchair. How Linda and Jane can ferry Sandy around single-handed is a mystery to me. Later I glimpse Linda having a push and the chair is the same height as her, her arms reaching upwards to touch the handles. That's as potent a symbol of friendship as you'll see.

I wheel Sandy into her vehicle, via an electric ramp. The girls suggest a morale boosting visit to Sandy's favourite tall ladies' fashion store. As Jane drives us there, with the vehicle handling no doubt differently with Sandy's enormous bulk in it, I get to talking to Sandy a little bit more about her blue moods. I always find cars a strangely conducive environment for a candid chat. I think it's the reduced eye contact – with everyone focussed on the road ahead – and the engine noise helps too, drowning out any potential awkwardness. And the space in a car is usually pretty intimate, which is useful too. I am sitting on a normal car seat in the back, alongside Sandy, whose wheelchair is strapped into place by a thick rope her doppelganger Richard Kiel could chew through in about twenty seconds.

'Sandy,' I ask, 'do you think you're taking enough care of yourself? You know when one of these infections is coming, do you think you pull out all the stops to prevent it or do you think maybe you neglect yourself a little bit sometimes?'

'Oh I might neglect myself, but they take pretty good care of me in the nursing home,' she says, deflecting. I can see how she is a tricky customer when it comes to taking well-meaning advice.

'Why do you think you neglect yourself? Is it when you get a bit down?' I ask delicately.

'That could be, yes,' she says. Immediately changing the subject, which I've noticed she does a lot, she goes on, 'I need for them to let me have a ... I want a kitty cat in my room because I need the companionship. I don't like to be by myself all the time. And a cat would be something I could love and it could give me love back, you know?'

I catch Jane through the rear-view mirror throwing her eyes to the heavens. Linda, her and Nadine are somewhat weary of the cat conversation, which is a regular request of Sandy's. It's quite clear it would be impossible to keep any kind of pet in a nursing home and it's also not in any way

certain that, given Sandy cannot care for herself any more, she can take care of a little cat. Like her friends and carers, I don't want to be unsympathetic to Sandy's desire to have a furry companion. In fact, it's heartbreaking to think that the recurring theme in Sandy's life of being denied someone or something to love is manifest once again in this debate over her having a cat.

But the practical impossibility of this request and Sandy's refusal to countenance why it wouldn't work is a clue to her mental state. Sandy is extremely coherent and highly intelligent – she is a voracious reader and a consumer of tens of puzzles a day – but her grip on reality is on the wane. With her regular bouts of illness – as a result of, so Nadine tells me, variously refusing medication, fluids or even food – I think we are witnessing in Sandy a diminishing desire to still be around. It seems she's gradually getting iller, lonelier and sadder. I've seen it in friends and family I've lost over the years. An irreversible disenchantment with life itself is far worse for your health than any number of fags and fry-ups.

Sandy's mental fluctuations and her flashes of delusion and fantasy are having a detrimental effect on her body. As Nadine says, if Sandy gets an infection, 'that's a lot of infection'. When most people are feeling down and fail to take care of themselves, the body is usually robust enough to brush it off. Sandy's health has her on a shorter leash. At 7 ft 7 in tall, Sandy is already, at the ripe age of fifty-two, a walking physical miracle. She might easily have checked out a decade ago and it is a testament to her extraordinary strength of character that she is still here. But any amount of self-neglect in her case, could have rapid, dire consequences. This is what upsets Linda and Jane so much. They are already mourning the loss of their friend, because they see she has reached the point of no return. Yes she's wearing Shaq's tracksuit, signing autographs and going around in that monstrosity of a van. But behind that sprawling smile is an aching pain a whole litter of cats couldn't fix.

Wary of the cat issue taking over the whole conversation, I decide to move things on by asking Sandy about how much she profited from her celebrity status. A part of me wonders why, in the country which is the global entertainment capital, she isn't living in a mansion in Bel Air. She has had a steady trickle of work, doing public appearances and has indeed travelled the world. But here she is, at fifty-two, without a dollar to her name, her cash-strapped friends putting gas in her car. And yet she is one of America's more remarkable citizens.

'Sandy, how much does it get you down, when you think about your incredible title of World's Tallest Woman, that you didn't make more money from it, that you weren't able to capitalise?'

'I think I have, frankly. I've been really fortunate with all the help that people have given me I think. I do miss something

though. I miss working at a job. I was a secretary and I kind of miss working. And I felt like I was at least accomplishing something in life, you know.' In her late teens she did indeed have a job locally in administration. Another aspect of normal life that we all too readily denigrate, but which someone in Sandy's position craves.

We arrive at the mall and unload Sandy from the car. People glance over at her as Linda wheels her into the shop. Fun ensues as Sandy grabs various items and holds them up to her chest to see how they would fit and whether the colour would suit her. She's in her element. This is something 'normal', that she gets to do. It's great to behold. Other female shoppers pop over to greet Sandy. She is gracious as ever, partly because I think she enjoys it.

Jane picks up a pair of trousers and shows them to Sandy.

'Those will be shorts on you!' she says and laughs.

'Short shorts,' she replies dryly.

A short, brown-haired lady in her forties comes up to Sandy and shakes her hand.

'Hi there, my name's Elisa. Nice to meet you; I didn't know that we had somebody so famous and special living nearby.'

Sandy smiles sincerely. 'Well, hey there,' she says.

'How are you?' Elisa asks.

'I'm doing just fine,' she replies, ever the professional. The public don't want to hear about there being no big husband to lean on, no money and worst of all, no kitty cat...

Another lady, fair-haired, thirties, comes up to Sandy. 'Hi,' she says.

'Hi there,' says Sandy.

'I'm Michelle.'

'Michelle, I'm pleased to meet you,' says Sandy robotically.

'You too.'

'My name's Sandy,' she says, knowing they know she's Sandy. Shelbyville is not a big town. I always think it's odd when very famous people introduce themselves with their full name, like 'Hi I'm George Clooney, good to meet you.' I think if I was George Clooney, I would feel I've passed the point of needing to name check myself. I'm sure in George's case it's characteristic of his charm and humility and it's why we love him. But it still sounds a bit odd.

'Sandy,' I say, 'you've had a lot of attention since you got into this store, do you enjoy being a celebrity like that?'

'It doesn't bother me, I think it's nice when people come up and say hello.' She's quite the politician and that's as close as you'll get to a 'yes' from her. Clearly, as the girls told me early on, it's an important daily boost for her. A catalyst to keep on going and, as they explained, it's really all she has left.

Sandy continues on the theme of public attention. 'I'd rather they would do that, come up to me, than people stand and ... wait a minute, wait a minute.' She is suddenly side-tracked by a green necklace she spots on the jewellery rack.

It is a long string of beads and stones, all various shades of green. It is a pretty item.

'Oh I forgot; I got too close to the jewellery counter,' says Linda ruefully.

'Oh isn't that pretty? I like that,' says Sandy admiringly. She then puts it back as a matter of course. Anything nice that she'd love to have – she can't have. It's something of a metaphor for Sandy's life and it hurts me to witness this tiny moment of pathos.

As we continue to browse, I ask, 'Do you know of any other people out there who are very tall and growing?'

'Wasn't there a woman from China? Is she still alive, that lady from China?' asks Sandy, loudly to her wider entourage of Linda and Jane.

Linda replies, 'Yes.'

'Is she?' I ask.

'Yes as far as I know she would be my closest competitor,' says Sandy, giving me a warm and knowing grin.

'Is she taller than you are?'

'No,' she replies, firmly and swiftly, her lips pursed. She isn't having any of it.

'So how would your life change if today it was announced that there was somebody in the world taller than you? I think you'd miss that cache, wouldn't you?'

'I suppose I might,' she says, wanly. 'I don't want to say I'd be jealous but yes I would miss being number one. Yes

I might.' She is being very open and very honest and it's very gratifying. At various intervals, I've felt like I only got glimpses of the real Sandy. This larger than life persona and the constructed bonhomie of the public Sandy Allen was proving, at times, hard to get past. As I travel the world, in this incredibly privileged position of meeting all sorts of utterly unique individuals, I can't always hope that people will, on command, spill the beans about their whole lives, warts and all.

But what is incredibly important to me and what needs to happen to justify the time involved, the distances and the many litres of airplane tea consumed (with an occasional cranberry juice, just to break things up), is to feel some kind of connection with the person I've come to see. There is an unassailable truth to these moments of connection, and an authenticity that no amount of theorising, background reading and Googling will give you. That's why I go there. It can't be done online, or down the phone. This is a moment, in my unforgettable encounter with Sandy, that will stay with me. She has allowed the sadness in her eyes to come out and to share, honestly, the one attachment she has. Ironically it is her height, and the global scale of the fame it brings, that has both robbed her of an existence and given her one.

Then, with a small paper bag in my grasp, I zip up my coat and prepare to say goodbye to Sandy. I tell her what a joy it was to meet her, what an amazing person she is and how

she should please please take better care of herself because we care for her very deeply. Linda and Jane once again fire up with a Mexican wave of vigorous nodding. Sandy says, a touch unconvincingly, that she will. As I kiss her on both cheeks (I've got the hang of this now), I bid her farewell. I think she enjoyed the visit and I think she took a liking to me, which was genuinely thrilling. Before I go, I hand her the paper bag. Inside is the green necklace. She cries and I get another lovely hug from the tallest woman in the world.

As I head to Indianapolis airport, wondering whether the continued heavy snow will ground my next flight, I return to the burning issue of whether Sandy is indeed the tallest female on the planet. I wasn't going to break it to her, and frankly I'm not sure she should ever find out, or needs to, but there's a good chance the woman in China she mentioned at the shop is indeed taller that she is – I've heard by around two inches.

I have to pretend to Sandy that I'm off back home to see the kids she's taken a shine to from the photos on my phone. But I'm not; I'm off to meet somebody on the other side of the world, whose story might blow Sandy's out of the water.

PART 2
The World's Tallest Woman
Yao Defen's story

Yao Defen is not listed in *The Guinness Book of Records*, the only guide in these matters. As I say goodbye to the USA, and hello to China, it strikes me that that's something the world's geopolitical and economic pendulum is doing as we speak. It's good to know I'm in step with the direction of history ...

I'm travelling 7000 miles from Indiana to Shanghai. My fixer has discovered that the woman in question, Yao Defen, is living in a small agricultural town called Shucha, four hundred miles east of the booming metropolis. And there's no means of contacting her directly. Word has come back via a villager that although she would accept a visit, like Sandy she is in very poor health. It feels like quite a wrench going from meeting Sandy in a homely patch of rural America, where I could banter with her in my own language, to a bleak Chinese town where the language was the first on a long list of things that was alien. Shanghai itself is a pumping, thumping hive of capitalist activity. The imposing quayside area is a late-twentieth-century take on Manhattan, with myriad skyscrapers and unendingly vast shopping malls. A visit to Beijing brings similar confusion about what China is. This controlling communist state is now, second to America, the biggest proponent of the capitalist dream. And at this rate, China will be number one, probably by the end of this sentence.

Though China's cultural and political contradictions in Beijing are illustrated in the architecture, with branches of Starbucks and McDonalds within a hair's breadth of Tiananmen Square and other iconic communist party buildings, in Shanghai, there are no such contradictions. It's not East meets West. It's West meets West. It's all glass, chrome and stainless steel. The old part of Shanghai, with its capacious markets and food courts feels like nothing more than a quaint throwback. It's all about Gucci, Prada and Armani. And if you like a big, modern urban backdrop, Shanghai is your place. It's a beautiful city, clean, exciting, cultural and it's actually statistically impossible to eat badly there. A boast I'd love to be able to make about any number of UK cities.

But I'd better not get used to the vertigo-inducing glamour of Shanghai itself. Because T, my redoubtable fixer, and I are going to spend a very bumpy day bouncing around in the back of a minivan. Bouncing alongside T and me in the back of the van is a pair of specially made shoes for Yao Defen, from a sympathetic and generous shoemaker in Germany. The box housing the shoes is massive, which was an auspicious sign. It suggested that if I'd come all this way to meet someone taller than Sandy, I might not be disappointed.

We arrive in Shucha, a dusty town, buzzing with tractors, cars and trucks, carrying all manner of life – construction workers, schoolchildren, cattle, ducks and goats. In fact, it appears that here, anything with a pulse can be packed into an overcrowded vehicle and treated to a long trip on a potholed road, without the merest suggestion of a seatbelt, a working radio or, God forbid, air conditioning.

I'm a sucker for busy places. Born in London, I'm a crowd junkie. The silence and intense darkness of the countryside at night make me nervous. So although this place ain't Shanghai, it's still noisy and vibrant. It has a buzz that comes with too many people in too small a place. Which, by the way, is the key characteristic of a good party. But this isn't a party town. It's just people going about their business, trading their wares and making their own small contribution to China's economic revolution. It's not a picturesque place. The local nature is unremarkable, just well-exploited field after well-exploited field, housing crops and cows and the like.

There are plenty of markets and shops, but in terms of turning the heads of any passing trade, if the products in these stores – fruit, veg, tobacco, dresses, mobile phones – don't draw you in, nothing else will. A cafe I stop off at for some burningly hot green tea and a cake is friendly enough, but if it wasn't for the box of cakes at the entrance, it might well pass for someone's front room. Desperate for a toilet break before meeting China's answer to Sandy Allen, I pop to the rear of this establishment, only to discover I will be evacuating into a hole in the ground, centimetres from a goat with very accusing eyes.

The local who'd made the initial contact has agreed to introduce us to Yao Defen. Wearing several coats, all on top of each other, he has a ruddy complexion and keen, rapid eyes. He seems to be the guy to know in the town. If you were in a Bond movie, he could get you a meeting with 'the Fat Man'. I'm not in a movie, and he's getting me a meeting with the tall woman. Maybe the tallest one on the planet.

As we walk along the battered pavement, passing a parade of small shops on the way, the crazy height differential between this tiny, tri-becoated man and myself is comical. With my 6 ft 4 in, I'm worried I might be stealing Yao Defen's thunder in this town, as people spin round to take my unfeasible height in. Here, you only need to be about six foot in height to make it into the local paper – 'tall freak visits China shocker'! I then remember Yao is allegedly well over a foot taller than me, so there's very little thunder stealing to be done I suspect.

'How famous is Yao Defen in this area?' I ask the man. 'Is everyone here proud of her height or do they think she's strange?'

'We find it a bit strange because she's a lot taller than everybody else,' he says.

'Is she liked around here? Is she a friendly, familiar face?'

'We are a little bit intimidated by her; she doesn't really have a lot of interaction with the local villagers.'

Hmm. The plot thickens. This doesn't feel like Sandy, who is a celebrated local celebrity. He tells me that a tumour on Yao Defen's brain which had triggered her abnormal height – exactly what happened to Sandy – was now threatening her life. Apparently the only person available to care for her is her mother. It seems Yao isn't lucky enough to have a Linda or Jane.

We swing a right on to an unremarkable side street at the end of which is a remarkable mountain. It's a street like any other in this neighbourhood, a little scruffy, but bustling with life. I don't know why I'm looking for visual evidence that Yao Defen lives here – there's unlikely to be an unfeasibly tall front door, or indeed a blue plaque on the wall, stating that a very tall woman lives here. I suppose it's just that the resident of this street may well be the tallest woman in existence and someone whose physical scale deserves not only a place in the record books but also in the history books. As a female giant she may be a phenomenon that history has no record of hitherto in the human story. And there really is no fanfare about this residence whatsoever, which does say a lot about how the modern world views people who are physically extraordinary. If the likes of Yao and Sandy had lived in the Victorian era, they'd have been bigger than Madonna.

As my 'man in Shucha' guides us to Yao's property, I am confused as it looks like a shop. There is a glass front with metal shutters on the outside and shabby, yellowing curtains on the inside. A late-middle-aged lady with bad teeth and greying hair slides the door open. She is dismissive and unfriendly as she mutters something in Chinese to my two colleagues. They are responding, seemingly defensively.

This busy pensioner has grabbed a broom – a metaphorical and literal crutch for her, it seems – and is sweeping the front of the property furiously, each whip of the bristles on the ground, another dismissive gesture aimed at this freakishly tall Englishman coming to see her freakishly tall daughter. One of her front teeth juts out over her lower lip, creating the permanent impression that it is falling out of her mouth. This woman is literally long in the tooth and if my journey was about meeting the world's most noticeable alignment of front teeth, my trip would not have been wasted. Happily, my search is for a rather grander and rarer physical quirk, the owner of which appears to be reclined in the back of the room. I only catch the slightest of glimpses, and all I can see is miles of trouser. I don't think I'm going to be disappointed.

My ability to actually meet her is, I discover awkwardly and at the last minute, not a given. It has long been agreed with my fixer and the man who knows 'the Fat Man' that Yao Defen would welcome a visit, to draw attention to her physical plight – she too not surprisingly has health issues.

On arrival, however, I am greeted with the request for money. Hard currency. Fithy lucre. 'A bit of scratch', as my old boss in radio Bill Ridley used to call it. Now this is a tricky area, because I don't want to get sucked into participating in chequebook journalism. Ethically it's compromising and not good for the ecosystem of journalism. If everybody charged money for their story, we'd be even further from the truth about the world and the people in it than we already are.

In the past, people have asked for money prior to my meeting them and I've had to pass on the opportunity. In some ways it's helpful that money exists as a temptation because if somebody extraordinary, like Minka or Sandy, is willing to meet me for not a penny it suggests they want the world to hear their story. They might want to be seen by a wider public, be understood or it may just be that they are happy that someone is interested in them and are thus not inclined to spurn my attentions. If, however, people will only grant me an audience for money, then apart from making the whole affair feel like a transaction, which is the opposite of why I've come all this way, it also raises the spectre of people prostituting themselves and their story for a fast buck.

This is all well and good in a nice air-conditioned office in London or Manchester or Glasgow. But I'm in bloody China. I've come from Indiana. Do you have any idea how hard it is to get from Indiana to China? There is very little call for the good people of Indiana to go directly to China and vice

versa. And I arrived thinking this was a sure thing and a done deal. It's unsettling to feel the goalposts lurch so dramatically on arrival here. And given that I am in a place I didn't know existed a week ago, thousands of miles from home I feel strangely vulnerable. How much is she going to ask for? Do I have it? Should I pay it? Should I pay it all? Or half of it? Or none of it. I'm in a real pickle. But it's not a jolly 'shall we have Martini, or shall we have absinthe?' pickle. It's a lonely, aching pickle. I have precisely 100 per cent to lose if I go now. But what's to be gained from paying? Surely it will make it the wrong kind of encounter and thus counter-productive. Sandy gave of herself. She shared her beautiful, stubborn soul. She smiled her Richard Kiel smile and I like to think we left friends. None of this would have happened if she'd asked me at the outset whether I was paying cash or credit card. It's like sex. Sex is sex. But if you are paying for it, it's different. Massively so.

I go for a tea with T, mainly so I can write that sentence months later in a book. We go back to the cafe with a trench for a shitter. I'm virtually a regular there now. After a lot of discussion, I face the glaring truth that we have to go back to Chez Defen and we have to ask what kind of fee would be acceptable. T explains to me that Yao Defen is known for being rather canny about money and that a number of media organisations have stumped up a bit of scratch and sometimes rather more than a bit of scratch for an hour of her time. T also explains that Yao doesn't have a job, or enough money for the kind of medical care she requires. As delicately as she can put it, T explains that she needs the money and she is keen for people to know of her plight. Not the kind of moral mandate I was looking for, but enough to make me swallow my pride and my tea and return to Yao and her mono-toothed mother.

Returning to her home, a lengthy set of negotiations play out between what feels like about ten people. Key to the negotiations is Yao Defen's mother who, based upon her tenacious performance representing her daughter, could fairly be described as the Chinese Max Clifford. However, Yao's deep, booming voice in the background (fractionally deeper than Sandy's which is saying something) suggests that although her mother is the attack dog, Yao is in charge. We settle on a hysterically large fee – £800. As I hand over the readies, I comfort myself with the knowledge that this should keep the jobless Yao in her essential medication for the foreseeable future. By the looks of her living environment, it won't be wasted on any frivolous luxury items.

Yao Defen is living in a room no larger that your average British bathroom. The interior is tatty and colourless. There are no pictures on the walls or other cosmetic home comforts. There is a large single bed that even I'd find a bit cramped, a balding rug on the concrete floor and next to the

bed, a side table containing a couple of jars of prescription medication and the perennial object in any Chinese household – a rice cooker. So this unique citizen of China (and think of the odds of being unique and standing out in a population of a billion people) is living in one of the smallest homes I've ever entered. It's quite clear Yao Defen and her mother are hovering around the poverty line and though always tragic to behold, it is particularly so here, given the uniquely challenging circumstances for Yao and an ageing mother who has the unfeasible task of caring for her.

The first thing I notice about Yao is that she is considerably younger than Sandy – thirty-six years old – and it shows in her unlined, massive face. And she is very beautiful, her maxed-out features expanded to hugeness in a forgivingly proportionate way. She has long, ruler-straight dark brown hair, bunched together girlishly in a band, large brown eyes and a pale-mustard complexion betraying the lack of sunshine or fresh air it comes into contact with. She is wearing clothes that look tailor made for a giant teddy in the window of Hamley's toy shop. Long, cheap polyester trousers and an unendingly long tank top.

I am coming to terms with her vastness in every aspect of her body, to the extent that she makes Sandy look like she belongs in the same physical ballpark as the rest of us. Yao is in a league of her own and unlike my encounter with Sandy, I'm not finding it so easy to move on from how big she is.

Sandy is massively tall, but Yao truly merits the term giant. She is straight out of a children's fairytale and being in her company, seeing her smile and realising she is just another human being like you and me doesn't get away from the fact that she is supernaturally big. She might just be a bit bigger than Sandy, but there seems to be a gearing effect in terms of her scale with that extra inch or two. Her hands are enormous, her legs are broad and tumultuously long, her torso goes on for miles and her face, as mentioned, is huge, like a large oval painting. Even next to Sandy, she is a separate species. Mythically large.

As is an all too familiar sight, she is reclined on her bed. Not actually ill as such, but just too large to get up. At first glance it's a joyless existence for Yao. Her humbled, cramped surroundings and the fact that apparently she can only sit up for one hour at a time.

I am very lucky, as she chooses to spend a small portion of that hour with me. Watching her get up from her bed is a truly amazing sight to behold. Seeing her acreage of upper body slowly rise from its reclined position is the kind of truly surreal image that even the fertile mind of Terry Gilliam couldn't dream up. As she reaches the sitting position, which takes several painful minutes, it's like she's standing, given the length of her upper body. She sways on her bed, like a massively large lifebuoy bobbing about on the water. I am standing, she is sitting and in spite of that she and I

are almost eye to eye. My head is craned up as far as it will go to make eye contact with her. After a few minutes I am experiencing the biting irritation of a crick neck. It's utterly dumbfoundingly extraordinary for me to experience this kind of role reversal.

Settling myself and hoping my heart will return from my mouth back to the centre of my chest as soon as possible, I decide to get to the bottom of Yao's financial tenacity. The tenacity doesn't end with the deal being made and the money being handed over. Every so often during our encounter, she stops the conversation – quite abruptly – to lift her pillow, under which the pile of notes are stashed and she begins to count them out lovingly. She is clearly thrilled to have all this cash in her possession and I think the regular counting of it is the pecuniary equivalent of pinching yourself. I have been tipped off prior to our meeting that it is born from some fairly bad experiences.

'So Yao, we had quite a battle over money just there. Have you been ripped off in the past, exploited?'

'Yes I was,' she begins. Her hands are bent, palms down, flat on the bed, stabilising her vast upper frame, rather in the way fire engines and heavy trucks have hydraulic metal jacks that come out from the side of the vehicle and jam themselves onto the road surface. There's a similar thing going on with Yao's arms.

'I was working as a performer in a group,' she explains, 'and they just locked me up in the back, it was appalling conditions. And I got into an accident and I was burnt. You can see the scar on my waist.'

And before you can say anything, Yao flips up her top to reveal her scarred flesh. It's a nasty, lengthy scar that looks to have chewed up several layers of her skin. Shocking though it is, it's eclipsed by the surrounding flesh, of which there is so much. This flash of midriff shows off not only her scar, but the several hectares of human flesh that make up her middle body. Her tummy is an expansive plane of skin and flesh. The scars look like they have been produced by the kind of rough handling usually reserved for neglected livestock. Yao, it turns out, has had a career as a performer, though the words 'career' and 'performer' rather dignify what was a process by which this vulnerable and, let's be honest, disabled woman was used, exploited and abused. It seems from the colour of her stories that she was ferried around by a circus, enjoying the status of perhaps an elephant or tiger, rather than a human being. At least a tiger can fight back.

In spite of her stature, Yao is a fragile person and a physically weak one. If you are pushing eight feet in height, nature has effectively hobbled you in every department of life. The notion that if you are a giant, you are therefore strong is just another sour irony. In a company of circus players, Yao, it seems was easily the most manipulated, physically and mentally. I listen in horror as she tells me that one particular circus impresario drove her to the woods, tied her with

thick rope to a tree and abandoned her for a day. For why? To teach her a lesson for not being compliant in her 'job'. Unscrupulous is one thing, but abusive is another. In terms of sympathy for Yao, I have gone from 0 to 60 in less time than it takes Jeremy Clarkson to get into a fast car, let alone drive it. Yao explains how she was ripped off.

'A lot of times I work for the theatres and in performance groups. They all take advantage of me a lot. They promise me something and they don't deliver. I'm very angry about that.' And angry she does sound, in her Chinese Richard Kiel timbre.

Yao had led an extremely sheltered life – she'd never been to school and had worked in the fields with her peasant parents until poor health forced her to stop. I'm imagining the lurching culture shock for her, going from an empty rural environment where she was known by about eleven people and thus accepted, to a place like Shanghai with its deafening cacophony of traffic and miscellaneous trading and its blinding skyscraper cityscape.

But Yao's journey at a young age wasn't just one of culture shock. As she travelled the countless miles from big city to large town to mega metropolis, she went from local odd character that everyone's used to, to freak. Nobody is a freak in their own home. It's a safe place, free of physical danger (hopefully) and free of judgement and prejudice. This was taken away from Yao and all I can behold here today, in this tiny box room in a town four hundred miles from Shanghai, is a woman who bears the emotional and physical damage her unusual body has inflicted upon her.

It begs the question, if you are physically extraordinary does that mean you have to go into showbiz? Are human beings so insensitive and unthinking that we require anyone who looks different to put themselves out there for our consumption and titillation? And as I travel around the world meeting such people, am I just part of the feeding frenzy? I have to accept that, yes, absolutely I am. But I know that my portraits of these amazing people are warts and all. I want to see their warts, but also ours. We are all complicit in various degrees of exploitation and judgement of unusual people. The tragicomic nature of modern celebrity is indicative of how the freak show has played out in the Western world.

We don't have sideshows and circuses featuring the likes of Yao or Sandy, but we do have page after page in our newspapers and magazines of Britney Spears slowly falling apart, and we've all got a front-row seat. It's only good copy if that person is a human car crash, as Britney was, as others have been. For us as consumers, because of Ms Spears's wealth and fame, this makes it a guilt-free freakshow. We've somehow, having bought the records, bought the right to watch someone almost die in the public spotlight. And others have perished before the flashbulbs of public attention, Marilyn Monroe and Princess Diana being obvious but compelling

examples. Amid the various conspiracy theories as to how we lost Diana, the one we're least titillated by or engaged with is the one that suggests that the blood is on our hands. We are the ones who doubled the newspapers' circulations every time she featured secretly photographed in her gym or on holiday. We fed the monster. The only ugly aspect of the public mourning for Diana, though sincere and heartfelt for most, was the whiff of hypocrisy. We deified and adored Diana – and we turned her into a freak.

I hopelessly move onto the subject of love. Having spent a good deal of time in this world of tall females, the question now feels like a polite one on the list rather than one which will get a fulsome answer.

'Have you had any boyfriends in your life?' I ask.

'No,' she replies quickly.

'Do you still have hopes of finding love?'

I almost feel disingenuous asking the question of this immobile, gargantuan human being. Am I being patronising even asking? The flipside is that to not ask is effectively appropriating her destiny and deciding for her that it'll never happen. In my own case, my hopes of learning to play the piano like Jools Holland, or speaking fluent Spanish around the table with some Andalusian locals, frankly isn't going to happen, but the hope it will belongs to me and it's something I have a right to be deluded about. You can also never say never for any human being in terms of what may happen in

Enhanced Minka, sitting between her 'business partner' Woody and me. Tagging along is their old friend Kayla Kleevage (*far left*), for whom the clue is in her name.

New balls please. Minka gives me a whipping on the court. But the real star is that sports bra...

Me and the crushingly shy Sheyla Hershey. Here, she's just one operation away from being the most enhanced woman in the world. If enhanced is really the word...

7ft 7in Sandy Allen and me. It's a new feeling for her to look up to anyone.

Me and 7ft 9in Yao Defen on her daily one-metre stroll...

After a tricky start, Yao Defen and I finally hit it off. Perhaps the £800 I paid her helped.

Mohammed Daad, father to 84 children, and me. I may look happy, but he's had me in this headlock for six hours.

Me and the Sheikh of Ajman, who is kindly sponsoring Mohammed Daad and his huge family. Moments after this shot was taken, he bundled me into the pool.

Daad and a tiny portion of his army of children.

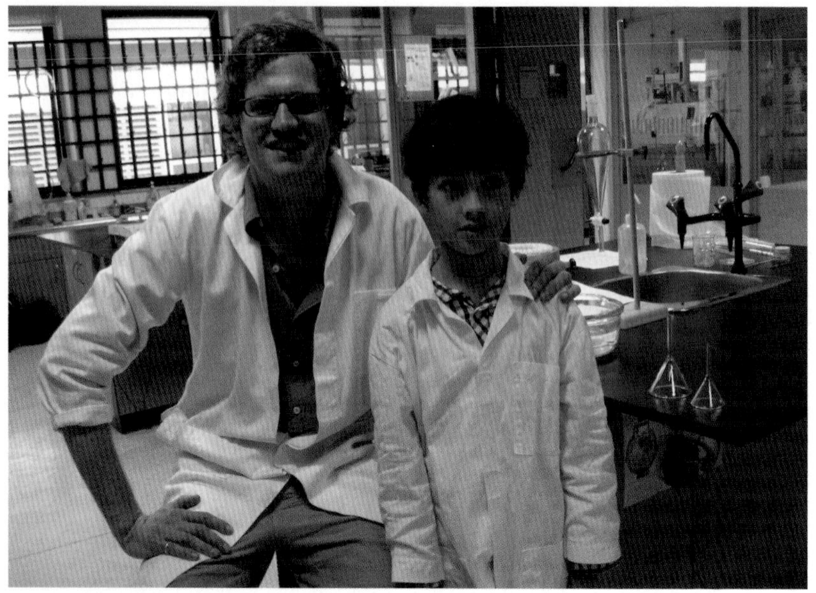

Chemistry genius, aged 8, next to chemistry idiot, aged 36. Ainan Celeste and me.

Khagendra Thapa Magar discovers the hard way his mother isn't ticklish.

He Ping Ping and his mum. A very nice lady, but sadly they only had enough ink for half her jumper.

Talk to the hand ... He Ping Ping wants his money from the bet that he'd never wear this t-shirt.

Didn't Khagendra's mother ever tell him about talking to strangers?

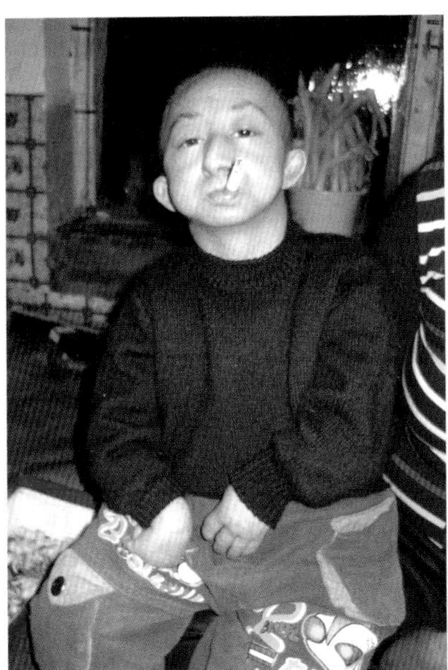

He Ping Ping lights up his fortieth fag of the day.

Khagendra in a typically joyful mood. He's just been told Spurs have scored.

Khagendra and me – the *real* Little and Large.

It's a barrel of laughs here in Inner Mongolia. He Ping Ping and I share a joke.

Larry Gomez, Hairiest Man on Earth. What's ironic, is that in this photo I haven't shaved for two weeks.

Cat Man, aka Dennis Avner, showing me the size of just one of his testicles.

their lives, particularly when it comes to matters of the heart. Love is like a mouse in a crumb-filled home; you can seal the building all you like, it'll get in if it wants to.

'No I don't think it would be possible,' she says, now blushing. 'I don't even think about it. I don't dare think about it.' She tilts her head down to her chest and giggles – unwittingly coquettish. Her tennis-racket hands are tucked between her legs, demonstrating her shyness at all this love talk. It's a matter of great irony that she comes across as a shy little girl, in such disproportionate contrast to her physical state. Her awkwardness and nervous laughter at this moment is very endearing. She is sweet and it's a delight to see this playful side to her character.

'You've gone all shy on me!' I say.

She laughs. In spite of the fact that an interpreter is diluting everything we're both saying and that we come from massively different cultures and that I'm a stranger and that she's a good 30 per cent bigger than me and that I'm probably asking all the wrong questions, we seem to have a rapport.

I strike with my big question – the one I've been saving up and travelled all these miles from Indiana to have answered. 'So Yao, do you believe that you're the tallest woman in the world?' I ask.

'I'm the tallest woman in the world,' she says with a power I haven't witnessed in her so far. She says it with the kind of certainty you would have if you were the tallest woman in the world. It's the sort of authority that that amount of size buys you. As she flails her endless arms around and as her voice reaches the level of a jet engine firing up on a cold Heathrow morning, I'm feeling slightly physically intimidated. I'm then struck by the thought that if she wanted to, she could kick the shit out of me. At one point in our encounter, while seated next to each other on her bed, as I make a jokey remark, she pushes me on my shoulder as a way of playfully rebuking me for my cheeky remark. Playful the intention may have been, but the force with which she struck me was utterly overpowering. It was like being playfully shoved by a combine harvester.

It occurs to me there is a contradiction here between the supreme strength and symbolism that comes with being as big as Yao Defen. As in nature, size implies supreme domination: the dinosaurs, but also vulnerability and ultimately destruction: the dinosaurs. Yao is herself quite a contradiction. She is the shy, coquettish girl, and she is the booming physical bully who knows the price of an hour of her time. But this is the same woman who was ritually taken advantage of and abused by her various 'managers'. I can only speculate that as I meet her, she is the product of what she has been through and with the help of her attentive and combative single-toothed mother, she is altogether more defensive and forceful than perhaps she once was. I guess it's survival. And it's no bad thing.

I'm glad she fleeced me for the honour of meeting her – so she should. She played the negotiations brilliantly, without appearing to do any of the dirty work and achieved 100 per cent of what she wanted and didn't even begin to meet me halfway. She may be poorly and living a very modest if not impoverished life, but she is in control of it now. There are no besuited ringmasters with sequinned waistcoats and top hats cracking the whip on her any more. And she seems in no doubt she is unique, which clearly adds to her sense of self-worth and hence her price tag. In that way, she's like a massive Kate Moss.

'Now you are not listed as the tallest woman in the world,' I continue. 'Why not?'

'Because I've never applied for the world record; because I don't know how to read and write.' I am shocked by this. I've obviously led a very sheltered life. I've met plenty of people with the slenderest claim on being educated, but for this famous, noteworthy, unique human being to be illiterate sets me back. It's another thing taken away from you if you are different, it turns out: an education. A physically extraordinary person in a school environment is variously an inconvenience, an embarrassment and a danger to themselves. So the alienation, the ostracisation and the curtailment of a normal life starts at school age. It puts paid to the notion that we all have a right to learn.

I am saddened that Yao is in this position, as if her size is not enough to bear. She cannot pass away those endless hours lying horizontal, with the comfort and escapism of a good book. And she cannot communicate with the world about her position, experience the fame and glean the income which might be a rare upside to her condition. I think the worst thing about illiteracy is that it guarantees to keep you where you are. Something that should happen to no human being, because that is a slow form of death. And Yao certainly lacks any noticeable *joie de vivre*. She is not well and not happy and the two are clearly interconnected.

I offer Yao a tiny bit of help in gaining recognition from the outside world. I suggest that I could independently measure her and tell the world that as far as I can judge, she is the tallest woman in the world. That is if she is ...

'Would you like me to measure you so the world knows that you're the world's tallest woman?' I ask.

'Yes,' she replies rapidly. 'I shall lie down then, because I won't be able to stand very straight.' She is receptive to my idea – which is a relief, as I can't really go away with just her word that she is the tallest. But first things first, of course. Yao just needs to whip the readies from under her pillow once again, to give them a quick count. Her fat, round fingertips flick through each note with the kind of speed and accuracy that would make *Bullseye*'s Jim Bowen proud. Once I've politely averted my eyes from this ritual – I always think there's something quite intimate about someone counting their money and I don't like to be in the room at these times – we get down to business. Yao begins the slow descent to a horizontal position. It's an image not dissimilar in scale, awe and engineering genius to the lowering of London's Tower Bridge.

I have a pang of guilt. I'm thinking of Sandy – someone I'd like to think became a friend in the short time we were together. What would she think now? Being in Yao Defen's grimy dwellings, with this tragicomic figure lying prostrate on the bed and with me brandishing a tape measure, it feels an unedifying process. Is this a betrayal? Is it even in Yao's best interests? My gut, nicely, gently expanded from years of eating Kettle Chips (salt and vinegar) tells me this is right.

If Yao isn't the tallest, Sandy reigns supreme. But if Yao is, that takes nothing away from Sandy. It doesn't take away the branded bus, the massive winning smile, the Shaquille O'Neal tracksuit, the double portions from Grandma's Pancake House. None of the coffee-guzzling patrons of that particular establishment will think any less of their 'leggy blond', if she's been superseded by a young woman in China. Sandy will always have been the tallest. She broke the mould. But the more I learn about these unique people, the more I see it is the person and the personality not the body itself which is the remarkable thing. I thought Sandy was remarkable, least of all because of her height. I certainly won't lose

one half of one per cent interest in or affection for Sandy if it is Yao who breaks the record. But if it is so, it must be told, otherwise Yao Defen is to be once again denied something she has a right to; this time recognition.

Yao is fully reclined, like a felled tree. There is expectation on her face. Not the kind of expectation an anxious sixteen year old has when opening exam results. Rather, the kind of expectation experienced by a prize heavyweight who knows a points win is just a formality. With the help of almost everyone in the room, I measure Yao Defen, using perhaps the longest tape measure in the world.

Yao nudges her head up to see if she can spy the result she's counting on. What a strange feeling, to have your body measured for anything, let alone a world record. I am reminded of that fantastic scene in *Carry On Nurse* in which a darkly suited bed salesman comes in to the private hospital room of Frankie Howerd, who plays a character called Francis Bigger, who is in for something very minor. Bigger is asleep at the time, so this funereal gentleman goes ahead and measures up the mattress anyway. Bigger is stirred from his slumber only to see what he thinks is his body being measured up for a coffin. Classic *Carry On* chaos ensues.

The tape measure hovers around her feet. As I stretch it, the tape shows 7 ft 5 in, then 7 ft 6 in. Could it be a tie? How great would that be? Then Yao could come over to Shelbyville and both extraordinary women could order out from

Grandma's and enjoy the unparalleled care of the redoubtable Nadine. This is of course madness and something tells me this tape measure has a way to go. It goes past 7 ft 7 in. Sandy's out. And she must never know. And frankly doesn't need to know. My thumb slides up to 7 ft 8 in, 7 ft 8½ in. Oh my God, this woman is a magician's trick. She just goes on and on. Finally my thumb and the bottom of her feet meet at exactly 7 ft 9 inches tall. Insane. This woman has beaten Sandy at a canter. If beaten is the right word. I'm elated, shocked, excited. Yao is calmly victorious.

'Well, Yao, you are 7 ft 9 in tall,' I say. 'So as far as I'm concerned and based upon everyone I've met and our research, you're the tallest woman in the world. Do you feel like a winner?'

'It's a good feeling,' she says, though quickly adds, 'but my health is just not very good. Other people who are tall can at least play basketball or do something for their country. But I need the country to take care of me instead.'

'So what help has the state given you in your life?' I ask, assuming Yao, with her unique needs and vulnerability, is the perfect person that the concept of communism was designed to help.

'Basically they never helped with money financially,' she explains. 'They give me a little assistance, but if I say it honestly, truthfully they will be very unhappy. So I won't say anything.' We have got onto the subject of the Chinese state

and even in a private home this is not deemed something it is acceptable to talk about. This reticence to explain how little her own country has helped her has cast a darker hue over this already pretty gloomy affair. Sandy may only have been enjoying fifty-odd dollars at Barack Obama's pleasure, but at least she had the right and freedom to rant that it wasn't enough.

Here, Yao's 'outburst' has made the atmosphere crushingly awkward. The elephant in the room is not this giant lady, but rather the brutal meanness of the state in which she lives. Mum has gone into a tailspin, and is screaming doubtless expletive-ridden Chinese at her daughter who, let's not forget, is three times her size. It's a shrill, eardrum-piercing barrage; she sounds like a hyena vomiting the remnants of a not quick enough zebra.

'What's her mum just been saying?' I ask T, my fixer.

'Basically she was telling her off that she shouldn't be saying these sort of things. And actually she wants us to go now.'

While it's a 'good story' to discover there is this level of paranoia about criticising the state, I am not here to make a cutting-edge exposé of China, with the conclusion being that its government isn't very cuddly. This is something we knew; this episode is just a reminder. Furthermore I'm not here to get anyone in trouble – my journey is not about stirring controversy – and Yao has enough problems without receiving a visit from a party official.

Prior to my now hasty departure, I want to hand over to Yao a very special gift, designed, constructed and donated by a very kind-hearted German cobbler by the name of Georg. The gift is a monster pair of shoes. Fortunately Yao wants to make her once daily outing to receive this gift. Barely able to walk, Yao is restricted to one ramble per day. This ramble involves walking the short few steps from her bed, across the room, through the house's front sliding doors, to a stool perched just outside. This manoeuvre involves three or four of us and is the first time I see her actually standing. It is predictably astonishing and no amount of acclimatising in this world of tall people could have prepared me for it.

As she rises from her bed, and reaches a full stoop (these women haven't stood up properly straight since about the age of nine), she resembles one of those big inflatable cartoon characters you get on floats at carnivals, the upper half of her body bobbing, and swaying left and right, in exactly the same way. Her larger-than-life face, with its supersized features floating around the vast terrain that is her head, looks like it has come from the computer mouse of an animator at Pixar. Her eyes are two drops in an ocean of forehead and cheekbone. She's big.

She sits on her chair and her mother, pleased the conversation has taken a less controversial turn, places a table in front of Yao, upon which a soapy bucket of water containing

washing is placed. Yao puts her hands in the bubbly water and begins pummelling the various items of clothing, testing their resilience with every squeeze. I'm really pleased to see Yao outside, with the hazy sun coating her face in a warm amber glow and highlighting her genuinely beautiful features. She smiles, as a soft wind wafts along this unassuming side street. A few locals take an interest in this spectacle, reluctant though I am to use this term to describe any human being. But from the flashing of cameras and clicking of mobile phones, it's clearly how these passers-by see it.

This I have come to accept is the lot of any physically extraordinary person. The more extraordinary and out of the norm the characteristics, the greater the interest. For some insanely unfair reason, if you look absolutely different, you become public property. Madonna is public property, as is Barack Obama, but their fame is voluntary and frankly, profitable. When they want to nip to a Starbucks for a quick latte and a bun, it's a headache, but it's just the downside of a contract they entered into when they signed up for global public recognition. Yao did no such thing. However, she seems oblivious to all the inane gawping, snapping and waving, much in the same way the rarer beasts at London Zoo seem to be. I could swear, a gorilla I looked at on my last visit to said institution, literally shrugged his shoulders at me before showing me his arse and bouncing off into the distance. Too right.

It's time to leave Yao by now. I can see she is already tired from the day's exertions, and she probably wants to get back to her pillow and check the stash. It just remains for me to hand over the product of Georg's labours. I pass a box to Yao who takes it in her trucker's hands. She is smiling in anticipation. Who doesn't love a pressie? Even the formidable Yao succumbs to the disarming power of a gift. She ably wrestles the lid of the box off and reveals a pair of bright red leather shoes that are, ironically, the size of two shoe boxes. They are completely stunning shoes – the soft leather giving easily to the gentlest touch and the colour a gorgeous shade of red; if Dulux haven't already thought of this, I'd call it 'rosy cheek' red. And as fate, and Georg, would have it, this fine footwear has put a rosy smile on Yao's face. She is really pleased and I didn't know her face could produce such a capacious look of joy. The muscles involved have come out of semi-retirement to create this expression, and it suits her.

'So Yao, what do you think?' I ask, hesitantly, as I have quickly become wary of false dawns with this lady.

'I'm very happy and I see something very new and interesting today.' I'm not sure what she means by this, but have to assume my visit wasn't horrific for her. She goes on 'and I've never seen shoes so nice'.

She puts them on with the help of her elflike mother, who barely comes up to her daughter's knee. Yao and her mono-toothed mother are indeed a children's fairytale

waiting to be written. The shoes are a perfect fit. Georg doesn't mess around. German assiduousness and attention to detail prevails once again.

'So how do they feel?' I ask.

'Feels good. This is the best shoes I've ever seen. I'm really, really happy thank you.' She smiles sincerely. This woman doesn't get taken care of enough. To see the impact of a gift like this is very gratifying. She has responded warmly to this gesture and I'd guess it's made her day.

'That's great. And they really suit you,' I say.

She goes on, 'Because I love red; my clothes are all red.' Indeed they are. With mum smiling for perhaps the first time this decade, I decide it's time to go. I thank Yao and her mother, and make my goodbyes with a peck on the cheek for both ladies.

As I sit in a bumpy minibus heading back to the 24/7 *instatainment* of Shanghai, I am moved by the experiences of meeting Yao and Sandy and even Miss Edna, and of course the various caring souls who quite angelically look after them. It occurs to me that these women are rarities and though not classed as disabled, have unique needs that go well beyond those of the most infirm of our society. I wonder whether political correctness or changing fashions mean these kinds of people are no longer national treasures. Our absolutely right aversion to the culture of the freakshow has had the unfortunate consequence of consigning these people to the scrapheap. It's a bit like the environment: it's one thing not using that inefficient, energy-guzzling fridge any more, but it's another thing chucking it in your local canal.

I'd really warmed to Yao during our short time together. And she was the tallest woman in the world - nearly two inches taller than the current record holder Sandy. I hoped that the title would at least bring her more money so she could get the medical help she obviously needed, and some recognition from a state that fails to notice that she even exists. The more I make these journeys, the more I realise it is about extraordinary people, not extraordinary bodies. Yao and Sandy were quite the most remarkable people I've ever met. And though Sandy has now lost her crown, which Jane, Linda, Nadine and I are all agreed is not something Sandy will ever know, both these women are in a league of their own and I'm humbled to have met them.

It is with relief therefore that I embark now on my next journey which takes me into a world in which the participant is a fully paid-up, voluntary recipient of the term extraordinary. I'm in search of another kind of size: the world's largest family. Large families, last time I checked, are a consequence of two consenting adults, one male, one female, having relations, without protection, rather a lot. I'm looking forward to not feeling frustrated, sad and angry at how nature can roll the dice with someone's fate and how society judges them thereafter. I'm looking forward to

meeting someone who has *chosen* to be different, taking the road less travelled, and being all the happier for it. But when one man in the sands of the Middle East has fathered 84 children, is happy really the word ...?

CHAPTER 3

The World's Biggest Family and Me

Who's the Daady? Mohammed Daad's story

There's a contradiction in modern Western society about family. Many of our social ills – youth crime, teenage pregnancies, even drug abuse – are often attributed to the breakdown of the traditional family structure. At the same time, certainly in Britain, people who have large families – eight, ten, twelve kids or more – are considered a terrible drain on society. The tabloid press – a warts-and-all barometer of mainstream public opinion – usually vilify such families, particularly if the family in question is working-class and/or receiving benefits. Such people are 'scroungers' and 'layabouts' and 'breeding like rabbits'. All people can think of is the cost of all those school places, supersized bin collections and perhaps ultimately, space taken up in the cemetery.

As the UK population swells, our tolerance for larger families has shrunk. Recent population growth has come largely from immigration from the rest of the EU, and whilst the UK has historically been a set of islands largely made up of people who arrived from somewhere else, it seems this tolerance of new arrivals isn't extended to those that arrive in UK maternity wards. This suspicion of large families ties in with a growing phobia of children in our society. Just turn on your telly of an evening and you'll see an array of naughty toddlers, cheeky children and unsalvageable teenagers being straightened out by an expert over the course of a week, with the help of some video monitors and a very large stick. At worst children are portrayed as a disease, a contagion, and at best a necessary evil.

Apparently they have no respect, a teacher isn't allowed to lay a finger on them, they are spoiled, they know their rights and they've got tellies in their bedrooms. If you are to believe the primal howl of the media, children are the cause of everything that is wrong with this country. And I haven't even mentioned hoodies - the dark, shadowy, anonymous symbol of a criminal youth culture. This can't work, because my mother wears a hoodie when she goes off to the gym, and she's in her sixties. It's all a bit hysterical and kneejerk. Has nobody read a Charles Dickens novel? Many of the youngsters featured in *his* oeuvre were proper little shits, but luckily for them, there wasn't a fashion at the time for hooded tops, thus making it difficult to give them a unifying nickname based around what they were wearing at the time.

Even the Greens, normally an anodyne bunch with whom I passionately agree, are out to get large families. They are an environmental catastrophe apparently. Overpopulation is the single biggest environmental headache we face, so the theory goes. As a race, we consume, excrete and throw away. Just by breathing the oxygen and thus exhaling CO_2, we are bad news for Planet Earth. Just existing is enough to be bad for the environment. In a matter of unparalleled irony, this puts staunch environmentalists in the same ideological camp as the Chinese Communist Party, famous for their one-child policy on the family. So with all this bile directed towards the concept of children, then having the temerity to have many, perhaps more than ten, is surely a crime punishable by at the very least a period of imprisonment. But there are those that do, and take the hassle in the local supermarket and all those judging eyes, because that's the path they've chosen. My challenge is to find out why they have taken such a path.

I'm the youngest of four, with two sisters and one brother, my brother being the eldest. I personally loved growing up in what by today's standards is quite a large family. It was of course noisy and at times messy. Stuff was variously snapped, drawn on, eaten, spat out, defaced, refaced, pushed unwillingly into something and pulled unwillingly out. There was variously mockery, polite contempt and open hatred.

But we were brothers and sisters, all in the same genetic and social gang. We belonged to each other and while separate, we were together and while fighting, we were just moments from laughing.

Being the youngest is I think pretty jammy, because ultimately you get to watch your older siblings fight the good fight for the next generation - setting all the hard-earned precedents and bravely beating a path past my parents, to adulthood. I think being the youngest of quite a sizeable crop also afforded me the chance to watch any mistakes that were made and, on seeing the consequences, issue a series of notes to myself to 'never try that trick' myself. As well as my parents' undoubted contribution to what was a happy childhood, my siblings take a large credit. As 'the baby' (a moniker I'm still stuck with), they entertained me, fed me, tickled me, carried me, occasionally dropped me and ultimately fed me a steady stream of love and, more importantly, penny sweets. The influence from different siblings of different personalities, genders and ages is extremely enriching. I think there is a lot to be said for the idea that your friends form your character and help teach you about the world. But I think you can take the influence friends have and double it for siblings.

And there is also no emotional elastic limit with brothers and sisters. You can't piss them off to such an extent that they walk away. They can't walk away; even if they do go, fundamentally, they are still there. There's no contract to rip up, no pre-nup the lawyers can help you wriggle out of. Family is for life, whether you like it or not. It's this knowledge that gives the relationship a robustness that will survive any amount of physical or spiritual turmoil. Siblings *do* fall out, sometimes catastrophically so. But it's about the most repairable bond there is, because it's made of flesh, blood and history.

What I know about the world of large families is that it defies logic. And from personal experience of meeting them - whether as a schoolboy going to a friend's very full house, visiting my relatives' big families in Ireland or in my experience researching this - large families seem to work. There is something evangelical about people who have loads of kids, evangelical with both a big and small 'e' sometimes. For the different reasons that people have for opting for loads of kids, be it faith, coming from a large family themselves, ideology or a desire for control, the family unit appears to be as willing to stretch as the poor mums who have to give birth to them. These families, from what I've ever seen, function surprisingly well, with the children often incredibly happy and well adjusted. While you'd think there would be a nightmare of tears, vomit, grazed knees and biscuits ground into the carpet, the opposite appears to be the case. These households are often content and ordered.

The parents don't seem to be exhausted, indebted or at war with each other (unlike the rest of us). It seems to be that

if the marriage is a solid and harmonious one, then in terms of kids, it's the more the merrier.

Every time I've walked into the homes of a big family, I've felt there was a lot of love in the room. I think it's what happens when you multiply the already loving dynamic of a smaller, more modern family unit. If you have kids and love them and take the fact they will love each other as a given, then by having more, you are just increasing the love. And children don't worry about being five to a room, because that's all they know, and while they don't have their own telly, their own Playstation or their own anything, they have something far more important: each other.

But what about those people that start having kids and literally don't stop? And how many is too many?

Surely there is a tipping point, at which you literally have too many children, and it becomes counter-productive, or even harmful for the kids themselves. To try to answer this, I am back on a plane and on my way to meet Mohammed Daad, a one-legged pensioner in Dubai, who has fathered 84 children. It's my first visit to the United Arab Emirates, and as we touch down on the runway at Dubai airport, I'm aware of the heat before the plane door is even opened. Flying over what seemed like hundreds of miles of desert, I could feel the plane gradually cook as it was sandwiched between rising heat from the ground and the blazing heat of the sun. As we sit on the runway waiting to taxi to the relevant part of the airport, we slowly peel off the layers that were so useful in the UK. I can hear the plane's air conditioning going at full tilt, but fighting a losing battle. In fact as we file off the plane, the cabin crew eagerly start pulling the blinds down on the windows so the jet doesn't overheat to too great an extent. Now I should point out that the hottest place I can remember being in my life is the desert of Nevada, but compared to the Emirates at two in the afternoon, it feels positively chilly. As I make my way down the steps on to the tarmac, the heat literally punches you in the face. But having spent the first two decades of my life living in the rainy fridge that is Britain, I'm not complaining.

I've broken an impressive sweat over the course of the twenty seconds it takes me to get to the air-conditioned luxury of the airport itself. Now the answer to the question of how one could live or work in such a place of heat is quickly answered by air conditioning, which is of course everywhere. But it always makes me wonder how the hell people survived in the nineteenth century, when it famously hadn't been invented. I can't work or sleep when it's hot in North London, so how can a civilisation grow, develop and prosper in 40 degree heat? A drive in from the airport to my hotel gives me my answer – by just getting on with it. Most of the population waft from chilled car to chilled office to chilled shopping centre. But as I pass by mile after mile of construction sites erecting more unwanted, environmentally catastrophic

skyscrapers, it's like going back to the nineteenth century as I spy countless Pakistani and Bangladeshi workers standing out there, in the blazing sun, with just a wide-brimmed hat for protection from the sun. I can't imagine ten minutes in this heat, let alone a twelve-hour working day, hammering, chiselling, lifting, pulling and pushing.

The national dress here makes some acknowledgement of the heat, with long white robes the required apparel of well-connected males. The women, as always drawing the historical short straw, are limited to wearing many layers of black. As I drive through Dubai, I'm reminded of Southern Spain in the 1970s – a place where frantic development appears to be government policy and where there is a perennial sense that it will be alright 'when it's finished'. But coming from a town like London which took a thousand-odd years to evolve, with a fire, plague and two world wars in between, it's obviously strange to witness the almost overnight creation of a purpose-built mega-city. The skyscrapers are many and almost universally mediocre, dating slightly before anyone's got around to opening them.

These buildings are not about style, they are a statement. It's a message to the rest of the world: come here, we mean business. The iconic Shekh Mohammed, still a youngish man who bears a striking resemblance to the ex-footballer and now Ipswich manager Roy Keane, took the pragmatic view that, as Dubai has comparatively little oil unlike its neighbours, it should focus its energies on being a global finance and tourism capital. Something of a Middle Eastern version of Richard Branson, he's in charge here and he's understandably much lauded. His vision for Dubai, though not perhaps the most aesthetic or indeed green one, has been successful. There are millions of people from all over the world who now come here to do business, party and gently fry themselves on the beach. This is the new Emirates. New money, new media, new world.

Mohammed Daad is more old school. We drive through Dubai, one of the seven Emirates, into Ajman, Dubai's neighbouring state. Though prosperous too, Ajman hasn't got quite the gloss or wow factor of Dubai. An altogether dustier and less overdeveloped place, there are just pockets of the modern world, and the inevitable high-rise towers and unending shopping centres that go with it. Otherwise it's a flavour of the old world, particularly in the form of a series of magnificent mosques, public buildings, parks and monuments. My fixer Najib is a chain-smoking gem of a man, and I've got to say in pretty much every way, he cuts the figure of a 'comedy Arab'. In the movie of his life, he will be played by Omid Djalili. Boisterous, neurotic and highly animated, he is an altogether amusing character to whom I take an instant liking.

Chunky and red-faced, with a fag and chewing gum habit he can't shake off, he and I are an unlikely but no doubt

mirthful pairing to behold as we speed through the desert in his Land Cruiser. We pull up at a petrol station and I bomb it from the car through a tunnel of heat into the ornate shop, where I stock up on water, Coca Cola and chocolate for myself, and Wrigleys and Marlboros for him. I massively enjoy drinking Coke in these aridly hot places, far more so than on a rainy Tuesday in Camden. I think the intoxicating mixture of sugar, caffeine and ice-cold bubbles is exactly what the body is crying out for in this environment.

This pit stop is our last before arriving at Chez Daad. I'm overcome by the stultifying heat that even Najib complains about (I want to ask him why he hasn't got used to it, but hesitate as I can see he's enjoying his thirtieth fag of the day). The flipside of the heat though is that I'm very much appreciating the uninterrupted sunshine here, which is a fantastic source of energy, transcending any amount of lost sleep. We are off the beaten track now, surrounded by rocky, sandy terrain and the odd mosque and low-level housing development. As we jump back into the car, Najib fires up another cigarette and turns on the radio, tapping his hands hazardously to the pumping tune rattling out of the speakers. Najib and I are having our own little buddy movie here, hilariously incompatible, but sharing an unlikely kinship. As we reach our destination, he knows all about me and I know all about him, which is something of a burden I'll have to carry for my remaining years on Earth. He's certainly an easy audience, with even the least mirthful remark made by me being met with a penetrating, hacking laugh that could wake the dead.

We pull up at Mohammed's place, which looks like a collection of four plain white villas, not unlike the set of the popular Eighties sitcom *Duty Free*. While rather large, it feels like a modest place. It's not long before we run out of actual road and bounce around on a gravelly path, testing the Japanese-engineered suspension to its limits. Finally we come to what looks like the entrance bit. There are some young men, in their late teens, standing around in long, white robes, while smaller children dart around, playing with what looks like a massive chunk of rock – Nintendo Wii, eat your heart out. There are bigger ones standing in front of a crumbly wall, which has an opening through which I can see into a fairly run-down central yard, complete with an old sofa, a swing and miscellaneous children's toys. At a glance I can see perhaps seven or eight children, barely a tenth of Mr Daad's flock. On the way Najib gave me a clue as to how Daad has managed this without breaking any religious rules. Between sticks of spearmint Wrigley's, he explained that in the religion of Islam, you can have up to four wives. These can be replaced if you divorce one of them, or if any of them die. So it seems that old Mr Daad's got something of a wife conveyor belt going on.

As I get out of the car, I am met with friendly faces, all of which share that Daad DNA. Hands are outstretched to greet me and I'm made to feel immediately welcome. This is all the more reassuring, arriving in a culture so different to my own. It's at these moments that I feel freakishly pale, tall and thin; it occurs to me how strange I must seem, with my uncontrollable hair, chunky glasses and strange camp way of talking. Actually a stroll through the more diverse parts of London makes me feel this way. Najib snaps into action immediately, chatting animatedly and laughing with these young men, like they have been best friends for years; the beads of sweat on his forehead the only clue to the real labours involved in such bonhomie. But the bonhomie doesn't last long, as the Arabic voices take a graver tone. Though inclined to tune out when around people speaking a foreign language, something tells me I need to hear this. I touch the shoulder of Najib's, sweaty, too tight t-shirt. He ignores the hand that feeds him cigarettes and continues to have this altogether more serious conversation. What's happened? Has Najib insulted one of the boys? Are they upset with me, and my general look? And by the way, where's Mohammed Daad – the main man? Perhaps in congress with one of his four wives ...

I'm standing in the shade, but still burningly hot. I've quickly learnt that if you stand as still as a waxwork, you're less likely to sweat. Therefore I do not move a muscle and fix a steely gaze on Mr Daad's offspring, thus probably looking all the stranger for it. Najib finally springs away from the group to explain what's going on, translating what one of the sons has said.

'He's saying his father is travelling tomorrow,' Najib explains. 'Today morning he travel already.'

Wait a minute, my sense of time isn't great, but he's saying he's travelling tomorrow, but also today? Is Najib seriously trying to suggest that Mr Daad is travelling in both the present and the future? What's going on – is he not only the most fertile man on the planet, but also a fucking time-lord? What we know is one troubling truth: it appears that Mohammed Daad is not here. He is travelling, either now, yesterday or tomorrow. It seems he moves around the world with more of an air of mystery than an international gangster. But I categorically have to meet him. Of course, there are plenty of his offspring here, and spouses, but making a documentary about this family and not meeting Daad is like making a documentary about the Atlantic Ocean and not seeing any water.

'What's happened?' I ask.

'It's because his sister died.'

'Mr Daad's sister has died?' I ask, naturally shocked. 'That's a real shame. So he's not here now?'

'No,' says Najib, looking like he needs a fag.

'Where has he flown to?'

'He's flown to Pakistan because of his sister.'

'Pakistan?' I'm no geographer, but it's pretty clear Pakistan is not down the road.

'Yeah, because his sister, she did the accident there,' says Najib, still with half an ear on what the young sons are saying.

'Right. An accident,' I say, trying to take it all in.

'She die in an accident yeah,' says Najib, nervous from a mixture of shock and nicotine withdrawal.

'How long would a brother stay with the family when the sister dies?' I ask, like a news anchor who has run out of questions.

'At least, you know, one week,' says Najib.

'Really? At least a week?' I ask hopelessly. I'm obviously incredibly sorry to hear this appalling news and it's a tragedy for the family. But being selfish, it's also a big setback for my journey. In short, Ryanair don't fly to Dubai. So the cost in time and actual British money and an itinerary turned upside down is going to be pretty brutal.

Not knowing what's going to happen, I wish Daad's sons my sincerest sympathies for the loss of their auntie and disconsolately return to the air-conditioned chintz of my hotel. In this heat, a hotel is more of a prison than a haven, given that a stroll around the neighbourhood at three in the afternoon isn't an option. In fact, it's an amazing thing to behold when night falls. My hotel seems to cater for ex-pat British electricians and electrical engineers (small talk in the lift is a daily struggle), and is situated on the beach. Once it gets dark, the

place comes alive, with families promenading and teenagers knocking a ball around on the sand or even playing volleyball. At 10 p.m., babies that back in the UK would be in their third hour of deep sleep, here are bouncing around the place. This is their peak time and it's the first moment since my arrival that I can see how this community functions and that a community exists at all. It's a lively and bubbling social network which is hounded indoors during the day by a maniacal sun.

As I sip my eighteenth mango juice, it is with a heavy heart that I go online to BA.com and look at rescheduling my flight. I will be returning to London, biding my time for a week or so, and returning to sunny Dubai. On my way back to London, while enjoying Joe Pesci in *My Cousin Vinny* on the classics bit of the in-flight movie database, I have an aching worry that I've missed my chance to meet a man whose story was at the extreme end of the world I was exploring. In terms of making babies, this chap is the high water mark and while I felt I had a broad understanding of what might motivate the creation of a large family on a scale of ten or twenty, I hadn't a clue how you could ever want to have 84. If I don't get to meet him, I'll never find out.

I spend a few days at home, enjoying the comfortingly temperate climate that facilitated the creation of the biggest empire in history and the world's first industrial revolution. I think I'd probably give all that up for a little bit more sunshine and a tad less rain though.

Having been given the all clear on the phone by a husky-sounding Najib - and to think, he promised me on parting he'd quit the fags - it looks like a return to the Middle East is on. Startlingly and joyfully there is no dead sister. Wires were crossed and whilst Daad's sister was in an accident, it turns out she and her fellow passengers are all fine, recovering mainly from the shock. I'm obviously relieved for her and the family and have my first clue that Daad is a caring chap, having dropped everything, including his doubtless daily sojourns to the bedroom, to attend to his sister. I'm also pleased that I'm not going to be intruding on private grief; at a time of loss, nobody needs a tall, specky Englishman asking them why they have so much sex.

I am greeted at the airport by one of Najib's buddies - Hatem, an altogether calmer character. I'm going to miss Najib's nervous energy, machine gun laugh and erratic driving. I shall have to make do with Hatem's steady professionalism and near-perfect English. We pull up at Daad towers and how surreal for such a remote part of the world to be so instantly familiar. I even recognise the chunk of rubble the younger kids were using as a football. To go somewhere unusual and remote once is an accident, twice is plain foolhardy. This time I can be in no doubt the source of this river of humanity is at home. It's unmistakably him - all sixty-three years and one leg of him. Mohammed Daad is sitting, resplendent in white robes, on a bench outside his large home. I get out of the car and he raises one of his 1970s NHS crutches at me. He smiles and gestures to me to come over, as he rises to his feet, or rather, foot.

'Hello, Mr Daad', I say enthusiastically. 'It's great to meet you. I'm Mark Dolan.'

Before I can get any more words out, he reaches up to me and wrestles me into a hug, no doubt a well-rehearsed gambit performed on his many wives.

'Ah, I get a hug,' I say, astonished at this warm welcome. I had expected, in this traditional and strictly religious country, with its overt class system and social code, that our initial contact would be formal and stilted. Not so. I feel like I'm meeting up with a long-lost Irish uncle who's been in the bar for an hour too long.

'It's so nice to meet you,' I say.

'Yes,' says Daad, smiling, deploying perhaps the only English word he knows. It's one more than my Arabic though.

'Great and can I ask you, how is your sister now?'

'Better,' he says through the translating prowess of Hatem.

'So now, how many children do you have?' I ask. It's worth checking. A week is a long time in this house, it seems.

'Eighty-four.'

'Eight-four!'

'Yeah,' he says, like it's not an astonishing statistic.

'Congratulations,' I say. Bit late for that though, I suspect. The horse has sort of bolted.

'Thank you.'

'And how did you come to make so many children?'

'Seventeen wives,' he says with a cheeky grin. The same cheeky grin that no doubt makes the aforementioned wives relent in the bedroom.

'Seventeen wives?' I say, astonished.

'Yes,' he says, with a satisfied look on his face. His face is softly lined, his skin tanned and rugged. He sports a greying stubble, oceanically large, dark brown eyes and a set of rich, Denis Healeyesque eyebrows. Perched on one leg, his figure is solid but not fat and he stands at around five feet nine inches in height.

'Mm, that's a lot of wives,' I say.

'Yeah,' he says with a big smile, showing a set of neatly assembled, off-yellow teeth.

'I have one wife,' I say, 'which is enough.'

Ignoring this mild joke, he fixates on the number of wives I have.

'One?' he shrieks and literally doubles up in a fit of hysterical and incredulous laughter that goes on for what feels like half an hour. Just as his sheer amusement at the idea of only having one wife abates, he recoils again into another bout of belly laughter. As he laughs, he looks at me, pointing and gasping for breath, his beardy mouth open wide, his pink tongue dancing around inside his mouth. And when I say doubled up in laughter, I mean doubled up. His body is at half mast as he sways around, overtaken with the intoxicating mirth of my marital situation.

I am actually enjoying the reaction, as I have been so worried that this encounter would be a worthy and polite affair. So far, it is anything but. Having bonded as a result of my husbandly inadequacies, Daad invites me across his threshold and into the inner courtyard of his home. As I observed on my last visit, the house is a modest affair comprising four small buildings, forming a square around the courtyard. There are a couple of small, dark kitchens where any number of wives convene to cook up breakfast, lunch and dinner, as well as around four large living rooms which double up as bedrooms, with mattresses piled high up against the wall. There are no identifiable luxuries: I count two small televisions, one beaten-up radio and a single cooker. The place is inevitably dusty and a bit dog-eared, but strangely comfortable. I take a seat on a squashy sofa which sits in the centre of the courtyard. It's held together with gaffer tape, string and blind hope. It looks like it has been given its last rites by a number of families, before winding up in the home of one of the world's largest: a grisly fate for any sofa.

This time there are more like twenty children of various ages here – an improvement, but still less than a quarter of Daad's human empire.

'Hello. What's your name?' I say to one little boy who is about seven, with a shock of black hair, bright, expectant

eyes and a neat, small face which he has inherited either from his father or one of seventeen possible mothers.

'I am Hussain,' he says, giving me a very grown-up and serious handshake. I then go on to meet Mohammed (junior), Walid, Sultan, Adilam, Sara, Hanan, Farah and many more. Faria's special: being a baby I assume she is the youngest.

'Hello Farah, nice to see you,' I say with a big smile, doubtless scaring the living daylights out of her. 'Did you know that you're the 84th child in this family?'

'This is 83,' interrupts Daad dismissively. How foolish of me? I should have known that the endless flow of lead in Daad's pencil means that ultimately you have never met the youngest of his brood. There's either one in the oven, or one just out, freshly baked.

Smarting from this faux pas, I am filled in by Daad on his domestic arrangements. He lives in this house with his four current wives and their 25 children. The other 59 children live with his thirteen ex-wives in other parts of the UAE. Fifty-nine! I don't *know* 59 people. And this is a portion of the amount of offspring he has spawned. It's truly astonishing. Of course given Daad's considerable age, tens of those children are now married with families of their own. I should imagine that in a hundred years' time, almost everybody in the Middle East will be carrying some of this grinning, bearded Arab's DNA. And it may be no bad thing. I am very touched by his generosity of spirit. In spite of the language and cultural barrier, he is incredibly humorous, taking any opportunity to pull a face at me and include me in a puzzling Arabic joke. He is raucous and warm. If we were not in a culture that forbids alcohol, I'd be convinced he had a bottle of Johnny Walker up his skirt. He is also tactile. Now we know he is tactile with the opposite gender – the din of child laughter and rough play in this courtyard is proof of that. But he is tactile with me too, regularly picking up my hand, and holding it in both of his. The skin on his hands is warm and soft. Maybe he thinks I am just an odd-looking English lady with no chest and a bit of facial stubble, two drawbacks unlikely to deter him if his track record is anything to go by.

In truth, there is such an abundance of charm and humanity in this chap, it's little wonder he has enough love to share with eighty-odd children and all those wives. He has a big family, sure, but he is a big personality, with seemingly an even bigger heart. In what will be a continued theme of crazy honesty on his part, he insists on showing me his master bedroom, an invitation I had never expected to receive. The room is special in a few ways. Firstly it's one of the few parts of the house with air conditioning, so just standing in this space, I feel immediately more comfortable and less sluggish, which is of course how you want one of your four wives to feel when she's in there.

'This is my special room. This is my bedroom,' he says, smiling.

'Very nice,' I say.

It's eerie gaining access to what is effectively the factory floor of this vast family. It's like standing in a car plant in the dead of night: there's nothing happening right now, but you know in a few hours it will be a hive of frenetic activity. The room is plain, with yellowing walls, a wardrobe, a large rug and of course the bed.

'I am sleep there,' he says, gesturing to the bed which is large, low and square. 'And look, there's my TV.'

We are standing in the middle of this room, with Daad leaning on his crutch. It is a real shame that this energetic man is held back with this disability. He isn't overweight, but carrying all his bulk on one leg is clearly a strain. During my visit, he naturally spends most of his time sitting down and it doesn't really suit him not to be buzzing around. That said, his disposition is stubbornly sunny, like the weather. He lost his leg in 1999 in a car accident and it doesn't seem to have dimmed his spirit or his ability to make babies.

We make our way back to the courtyard where his four wives are sitting on the floor with their shoulders hunched over a set of ingredients that will make up our lunch. Ranging in age from mid twenties to early forties, they are cloaked in black and work with quiet, harmonious industry. Before I get a chance to meet them properly, I ask Daad how he remembers all the children's names.

'I don't remember all the names of the kids actually, but whenever I see the kids I do my best to remember the name,' he says.

It's a shocking admission. Imagine if you are one of the little boys or girls whose name has once again slipped the mind of your own father. My mother normally has to go through all the names of my siblings before she gets to mine, but she usually gets there in the end. I grew up safe in the knowledge that, broadly speaking, my mother and father knew what my name was. I suppose with 84 it's inevitable you will forget, but it's a telling indication of both the scale of the family and the price paid by the children, having so many brothers and sisters.

What can being literally just a number do to your sense of self, growing up in this humungous grouping? And how much of the children's development can he possibly have taken in, having his head turned in so many directions? I can remember my sons' first words, smiles, laughs, teeth and poos. Significant moments must have been lost on Daad, who was either back at the car plant hammering out another model, or attending to the many he had already created. Concerned as I may be at the impact on the little 'uns of sharing the parental limelight with so many others, I'm struck by how happy these children in a large family seem to be. It is a ready-made primary school and the children, of all ages and both genders, crash around the place, piggy-backing, playing an Arabic version of 'It' and generally doing their job of being children. The vibe from this home is abundantly positive.

The older boys are slim, handsome and courteous. Some of them are already working, in law, education and the police force. They play with their younger siblings and chat warmly with their dad. His one leg and sedentary position affords him a regal authority he probably had already. It occurs to me his disability and age are in fact an advantage for the children. Daad is around 24/7. He is a perennial figure, not only in the bedroom. How many children can boast that their father is around all the time, to tend to their needs, or to give them the occasional clip around the ear? As I grew up above a pub, although my parents were extremely busy pulling pints, buttering ham rolls and counting out pound coins for the till, they were in the building day and night. It was a real privilege to have that sense of parental presence all the time; it's a comforting and rare thing for a child. Daad's offspring have it too. He took early retirement from the military some years ago and is now able to enjoy the fruits of his coital labours.

I have a sense that this is a human being that just loves children and wanted to have as many as possible. I think this was perhaps his way of making his mark on the world. Not well placed in social class terms and not a wealthy man by any means, the way in which he has become king of his castle is by being Dad to so many people. These little cherubs

bouncing around on a rusty seesaw/swing construction in the middle of the yard are his crowning glory and his source of authority. Being a parent does earn you a certain sense of status in any culture. I'm often having to remind myself of my responsibilities. I am in charge of a couple of little people, and it's either a burden or an honour, depending on which way you look at it. But it's definitely a promotion in human terms.

And so no doubt this sense of status is something Daad enjoyed with his first few children and thus he kept on going. With more children comes more status, more little people who look up to you and trust you and love you unconditionally. Daad sits in the mid-afternoon heat and you can see he just loves to survey what he has created (with the help of seventeen willing partners). He is like a farmer looking out over a crop-rich field that was once a bog. He is proud of his family and he seems to love his life and his kids. It's an unconventional and some might say irresponsible way of doing things, but I've been in the homes of many more dysfunctional and unhappy families that comprised just a child or two, so I feel disinclined to judge this unusual lifestyle choice too harshly.

Also in the spirit of the rule that 'possession is nine-tenths of the law', similarly now that these children exist, who would deny their chance of life, something given to them by their mono-legged pater? Throughout these journeys I'm constantly having my prejudices challenged and my sense of what's possible broadened. Daad's situation doesn't feel wrong, in the context of the Emirates desert. My only nagging doubt is about the welfare of Daad's wives. It strikes me as they toil over lunch in the afternoon heat, that they might be the only real casualties of Daad's grand plan.

Although he's married seventeen women over the years, Daad has kept to the Islamic principle of having only four wives at a time, divorcing the others before marrying again. And the divorces are not down to irreconcilable differences, but rather to do with the state of their ovaries.

'I divorce them at forty, when they are stop giving kids,' he explains.

'So you divorced the women that have been married to you because they were no longer fertile.'

'Yes, that's right', he explains. 'In fact, I'm looking for a new kid, a wife actually, because I need to continue getting babies. By 2020, I want to have a hundred,' he says.

'By 2020 you are aiming to hit the target of a hundred children?'

'Yes', he says, without a flicker of doubt in his eyes.

'Now what gave you the idea to have so many children at first?' I asked, still reeling from the revelation about his biologically arid exes.

'You know Mohammed?' he asks.

'Yes,' I say.

'The Prophet,' he says.

'The Prophet, indeed,' I say. 'So you are very much following the Prophet Mohammed.'

'I like having babies, so I'm getting married as the Prophet Mohammed says.'

Hmm. I think Daad, with his many marriages and divorces, is following the letter of the law, rather than the spirit of it. And he does cut something of a renegade figure out here in the desert. I'm not sure he's the most pious character out there or the most socially compliant. I think it's his way or the highway, not only for his wives and kids, but perhaps even for his religion. He must be taking Islamic law with a pinch of salt, otherwise everyone in this part of the world would have vast families. In fact they don't. And even his older offspring with whom I chat, have gone on to have small families and don't share their father's desire to be king of the genetic castle. Daad, I suspect, is a bit of a one-off and a law unto himself.

Clearly one of the things that motivates Daad is the desire to be a record breaker, and it's an impulse which has already been profitable. On hearing of this famous man who at the time had sixty-odd children, the Sheikh of Ajman became a big fan and consequently began to support Daad financially, bestowing upon him a monthly retainer and access to a number of his properties, including the slightly dog-eared one he now calls home. It's an increasingly peculiar and

inconceivable story. Well, it's very, ultra-conceivable, if you get my drift, but it's just such a quirky tale that it smacks of fiction. But I'm there, and it's real and it's happening before my very eyes.

I'm pleased to hear about the Sheikh's involvement as it answers the question about the material welfare of these children, because even the most generous army pension can't feed that many mouths. And indeed the question of how so many human beings are accommodated is explained. But it's still a bizarre world, in which the local billionaire is charmed by your story and wishes to see you having more children. Rumours abound that the Sheikh, who to all intents and purposes is clearly a very nice man, is nearly as excited about Daad hitting a century as the man himself. I did notice there is a large framed photo of the Sheikh over the marital bed. It would appear the Sheikh's watchful eye is ever-present, to make sure he is doing his duty on a daily basis. 'You couldn't make it up' is a tedious cliché, but deserves to be deployed here. The whole thing is surreal and bonkers. But the comedy of the situation is tempered by my concerns for his wives, who don't even get enough time to earn the description 'long suffering'.

Goat is on the menu today and with preparations cracking on apace, I sit down with the wives on a step in the courtyard. In spite of their dark robes and headscarves, I can see a selection of variously aged faces, which are all compari-

tively plain. I suspect that Daad has a similar attitude to the female gender as Benito Mussolini did. The Great Italian dictator apparently took the view that 'a woman is a woman', thus explaining many of his plainer and stouter bedroom playmates.

'Nice to meet you,' I say to one of the younger, beige-skinned wives, the headscarf accentuating her powerfully dark, deep brown eyes. I reach to shake her hand.

'Ah no,' she says, resisting my handshake.

'Oh you don't shake hands,' I say, feeling like Prince Philip on a particularly bad day.

'No handshakes,' says Hattam firmly.

Once the dust has settled, I begin to help out with the food preparations, peeling various vegetables. The more we talk, the more they open up, expressing their fondness for Daad and the sorority implicit in their situation. They treat each and every child as their own, so the children effectively have one father and four mothers, they tell me. Though shocked at the fact that they appear to be doing all the work and have a seemingly subservient role compared to the men within the household, I have to be careful not to implicate Daad and his grand plan into this. The culture here is one in which a wife's role is very clearly defined as is a husband's and while coming from the West, I find it undesirable and alien to my values, it's not the story I'm here to tell.

As the final pieces of garlic are shaved down, and having been regaled by the ladies with tales of how they all muck in together with the raising of this brood, I cut to the chase. That they are not competitive with each other for Daad's attentions seems plausible, particularly when you consider what happens when one of them has his attention. If I was them I'd stick with peeling the potatoes and try to look as unattractive as possible and avoid eye contact at all costs. But what's less convincing is how satisfactory it can be to live with the prospect that you will be abruptly replaced when you are no longer able to deliver the big man his much-needed babies. They insist they are aware of this when they sign up to life with Daad. It turns out you really only divorce Daad on paper. In fact he collects wives as much as he collects children. All seventeen of his spouses are still a big part of his life, raising the children they have given him, from the various homes supplied to him by the generous Sheikh. The divorce aspect would appear to be purely an acknowledgement of Islamic law rather than his desire to 'ditch the older ones'. It seems in an unofficial way he does in fact keep his wives, but he needs to keep updating the squad if he wants more babies, hence his rotation policy.

As I say, it's all bizarre, and trying to identify any logic to it I'm finding impossible. But it's clear these ladies enter this arrangement with open eyes. It's the kind of arrangement that would give any self-respecting feminist nightmares, but it appears to be one not made under any kind of deception, coercion or duress. Astonishingly they are willing participants in his crazy game. Later Hattam subtly mentions to me over a sweet tea that these ladies come from deprived parts of Pakistan, where married life in the Emirates with a man like Daad is a considerable upturn in their material fortunes. OK, it's starting to make a little bit more sense now. It's his charm, perhaps, but in a sense they are also hopping on board the Mohammed Daad gravy train. And as they do, it's clear what their side of the deal is.

It's nearly time for a dish I can only describe as garlic goat, as they seem like the primary ingredients. I'm going to eat mostly white bread and tell myself the goat is lamb. I don't know why I need to do this, but it does help me get it down. Rural people complain that city dwellers have no idea where the meat they consume really comes from; in fact this is how I like it. I want to think that steak comes from supermarkets not from cows. Forays abroad, sampling meat from a stunned carcass on a spit is just not my preferred way of eating meat. For me ignorance is bliss, and being able to see the frozen look of horror in the goat's eyes moments before his neck is cut is, I'm afraid, just a bit too much information.

But before the meat fest, I just have time to quiz Daad one more time on his amazing life choices. Playing to his sense of humour, I begin: 'I have just one wife and you know it's exhausting to try to keep up with her demands in the bedroom. You have four wives. How do you do it?'

'I mean four it's not even enough,' he laughs, though I think he means it. 'But if there is a way to have more than four I'll go for it.'

'You're very much the Casanova of Ajman,' I say, playing to his sense of bravado. He laughs.

'So why is this?' I go on. 'Do you have special powers?'

'Everybody has to have sex. People tell each other that I'm strong in the bed doing sex.'

I'm not sure what this means, but it's clear he is astonishingly candid about his sex life. I strike while the iron's hot. 'So how often are you making love with your wife?'

'Afternoon two times and evening six to seven times,' he says. I wouldn't believe him, but for the din of humanity he's created in the adjacent courtyard.

'Every day?' I ask incredulously.

'Yeah', he says, smiling, but serious.

I need to go through this one more time. Because I'm probably not coming back. 'So you make love nearly ten times every day?'

'Yeah,' he says, tiring of my repetition.

'How is it possible?' I say, exhausted just thinking about it. Once again he laughs and I think I'm going to have to take his story at face value. While always inclined to intellectualise the life choices people have made, on this occasion, maybe

it is what you see. He likes having lots of children, he loves sex and he wants to break some kind of record. And perhaps that's all there is to it. He's certainly made it work. His family do not go hungry, I saw no evidence the children were suffering in their unique situation and even the wives seemed content with their lot. Sometimes you do have to take as you find, and Daad, from the first moment of my arrival, has been a joyful and dare I say it fatherly figure.

I too am swept along by his positive, warm humanity. As we depart, I'm treated to another of his lengthy embraces, thus sparing one of his wives for a minute or so. I'm shocked at everything here. The scale of the family, the number of ex-wives, the rotation policy, the Sheikh's involvement and of course, his stupendous libido. But I'll have to just take my shock home with me, and take the view that, as with so many of the unconventional relationships I've encountered in my journeys, against the odds it kind of works. It seems a family can look and feel like anything your wildest imagination could dream up. It can come in any shape and any size. It's just the core ingredients that are required to make it sing: respect, love, teamwork, compromise, tolerance, commitment and a fondness for getting busy in the bedroom.

However, having many kids *may* be a victory of quantity over quality. The opposite's the case for Valentine Celeste. He's only managed to sire two sons, something Mr Daad would find hysterical and lamentable in equal measure. I'm rather more impressed though, as one of them is the cleverest child on the planet. Or so the rather intense Valentine says. For that reason, it's destination Singapore; bring a change of clothing – you're going to sweat.

CHAPTER 4

The World's Cleverest Child and Me

Too clever by half
Ainan Celeste's story

Yes, I'm Singapore-bound, to meet the perhaps the most academically remarkable eight year old on the planet. He is already at university (I didn't feel ready at eighteen) and is in *The Guinness Book of Records* as the youngest holder of an O level in the world, the subject being chemistry; this he acquired at the age of seven. Impressive, given that as a fully grown adult male, I still haven't managed to get mine. It's a sore subject for me, in every sense. In spite of the best efforts and considerable patience of my brilliant chemistry teacher at school, John Older, it was a subject I didn't click with, to say the least. In my younger years, I wasn't a model student in any subject area, if I am to be honest. My motivation and focus picked up by the time I got to my A levels. But the

GCSEs were a bit of a write-off. I prevailed in subjects that rewarded a bit of charming waffle, cunning backchat and a twinkle in the eye. (There aren't many of those subjects, let me warn you, younger readers.)

On the upside, it seemed rather forgiving of the English education system that as you got older and, in principle, became capable of a greater and more taxing academic workload, your portfolio of subjects went from nine or ten (GCSEs), down to three (A levels) – brilliant! Obviously there was a vast amount more detail and scope within those three subjects, but I really bonded with the idea of going from nine to three. Look at the numbers: 9. 3. Do the math. Able to narrow my field of interest to French, English Literature and Politics for the next couple of years, I was academically extremely happy and even a bit productive. I then went on to cheerfully muse on the ideas of Marx, Engels and Thatcher – in that order – at Edinburgh Uni. (So now we go from three subjects, to one – double brilliant!)

But academically, until the age of sixteen, there were a lot of round pegs going into square holes. It's categorically, exclusively my fault, but I struggled with Physics, Maths and in particular Chemistry. Me walking into a chemistry class at any point in my school years was a bit like a pensioner attending a screening of *The Matrix* – yes they'll be in the room, and looking in the right direction, but that doesn't mean they'll take any of it in.

On the positive side, anything physical and literal in a chemistry lesson certainly caught my eye. Mini explosions, turning unnamed fluids a strange colour and mixing two friendly substances to create something nasty, was of course highly entertaining. All the chemistry paraphernalia was diverting too – the white coats, the goggles and of course the Bunsen burners. Ah the Bunsen burners. Those ingenious gas burners which had an airhole in the stem, allowing the flame to alternate between a stiff blue spire of gas to a wobbly yellow ribbon of fire. We were each equipped at school with a blue, lined A5 exercise book for miscellaneous notes, ideas, bits of working, etc. A laudable concept. It was termed a 'rough book'. Unfortunately, the rough book's true raison d'être was as cannon fodder for the Bunsen burner. Across a forty-minute period my class often managed the impressive feat of having at least one rough book on fire at any time, for the entire duration of the lesson; burning like the Olympic flame of academic insolence.

The vast majority of my colleagues were able to tear themselves away from their smouldering rough books and take in a wide array of fascinating knowledge pertaining to the chemical universe. Indeed I have contemporaries who have prospered brilliantly in that field, who are now doing their bit to make the world a safer, or more dangerous place, depending on whose payroll they are on. But it wasn't going to happen with yours truly. It was just Greek to me from the word go. It still sends a shiver down my spine when I think of myself staring hopelessly at the blackboard, my eyes glazing over during the mid-afternoon blood sugar lull, the countless arrows, letters, dashes, numbers, hyphens and symbols spinning together into a hellish blur.

So I'm off to Singapore to meet an apparently remarkable little boy who I suspect has incinerated very few rough books in his short eight years. As I fiddle with my iPod on the plane, the Steve Miller Band testing my eardrums, sipping tea that is as strong as it is tepid, I try to think what I know about Singapore. And I realise almost everything I know about Singapore comes from the 1980s BBC TV drama *Tenko*. It was a very successful show, featuring a group of Western female POWs in Japan during the Second World War. Looking back at it, I think the allure for a good chunk of the ten million people who tuned in was the faintly sensual appeal of a group of females being locked up together, perspiring heavily and having occasional fistfights with each other. I am later to discover the whole thing was shot at the BBC's studios in Elstree, on the outskirts of London. I'm curious about whose job it was to keep Stephanie Beecham and her comrades looking hot, in no doubt freezing UK temperatures. Was a bog-standard plant spray used? Or a damp flannel? Either way it was a convincing production – the brutality of the guards, the bitter jealousies and rivalries of the captives, and the interminable, damp heat. Who knew that all assembled were three-quarters of a mile from the M1 and a nine-minute walk from the nearest overground station? Now that was acting.

Well, I hate to surprise you, but on arrival at Singapore airport, I discover it's changed a bit since Stephanie and co. pretended to be there all those years ago. Modern, bright, vibrant, colourful, Singapore is an intoxicating treat for the eyes. And it's clean. Every inch of this place looks like it's been given the once over by Kim and Aggy off've *How Clean Is Your House?* It is spanking, shiny, glossy and big. The new stuff is properly twenty-first century: shimmering skyscrapers, jaw-dropping bridges and vast apartment developments. The old colonial architecture is plentiful too, offering a weighty backdrop to the precocious new Singapore. And speaking of precocious, I am now a matter of minutes away from the home of one Ainan Celeste, eight-year-old child genius. Or so I'm told. By his dad ...

Singapore is so humid, it feels like it's actually raining when it's not. It's balmy, it's steamy, it's moist. I think, all told, it's probably the worst kind of heat you can have. And Singapore has the look of a place which is always overcast. So there's a wet, suffocating gloom that grabs you by the throat and wrestles you to the ground. Not my favourite thing. I walk, damp trousers clinging to my legs and shirt glued to my back, into the plush apartment complex where resides young Ainan, his English-born father Valentine, Singapore-born mother Syahidah and younger kid brother (who apparently isn't a genius; I bet he burns loads of rough books). The apartments are post colonial in spirit. A set of tall, grand, white buildings, differing slightly in size and shape, but all on a very human scale, at around four or five storeys in height. They circle a large green garden area which is at the heart of the complex, and which comes complete with a bunch of palm trees and as many ground staff. It doesn't look like the dwellings of Singapore's super rich, but rather Singapore's solidly comfortable. I walk cautiously into a shaky elevator on the ground floor and head up to the Celeste residence. As the lift creaks under the strain of propelling my body upwards, I'm thanking my lucky stars I passed on the pudding on my last flight. The lift shudders to its destination, but not before leaving me a good fifteen seconds to worry before the doors finally slide open.

It's a sharp right out of the lift, past a view from on high of the grounds, and to the next front door of my trip. Even though the vast majority of my visits to various individuals' homes are official and pre-arranged, I always feel slightly like a doorstepping newspaper hack. I ring the bell, and hear the sounds of stifled chaos as those inside go into a last-minute panic, prior to opening the door. This is a syndrome that I think affects all human beings. Even when you are *expecting* a visit, there's something about that doorbell ringing and the blurred figure of the visitor peering through the cloudy glass that makes you want to make them wait, so you can do something unnecessary like puff some cushions or straighten a pile of books. There's an unspoken rule – you have about thirty seconds in which to keep someone waiting, because they don't know that you are on the other side of the door, inches from their becoated bodies. For all they know, you are on the loo upstairs finishing a long-anticipated shit. But after those thirty seconds, you are in the danger zone. The only way to buy another thirty is to shout 'one sec, one sec!' You need to shout this in a way which is so shrill and panicky, that it seems you are completing a task which is gravely important and which you physically cannot neglect to finish, otherwise death or serious maiming may occur. When they start wandering around outside the property, possibly to peer through the living room, it's game over.

After the release of a nexus of locks – who says there's no crime in Singapore? – the door swings out. Enter, stage left, Valentine. A relatively tall six-footer with a Lego-man lid of brown hair, fullish Billy Bunter figure and with the overall look of a thirty-something school prefect at a sporty but academically pedestrian public school in the English countryside.

'Hello Valentine,' I say.

'Hi Mark.'

He's been expecting me. There is a stiffness in his posture, suggesting he's prepared for the worst.

'Lovely to meet you sir,' I say. He's a posh Englishman, so within three seconds I've knighted him.

'Lovely to meet you too,' he says graciously. He likes the knighthood; OK, we can build on this.

'I'm so excited after all this time,' I say.

'You've broken the house rule,' he replies abruptly.

'What's that?'

There is a tense second or two. Holy the Lord fuck. What have I done?

'You're taller than me.'

My relief is palpable. He's doing jokes. This is supremely encouraging. I engage in the conceit.

'Oh no I've burned my bridges already,' I say, 'and I haven't even crossed the threshold!'

He smiles.

'Now do we have a shoes-off house here?' I ask.

'Yes we have.'

'That's why the country's so clean,' I mutter. He's out of earshot at this point, heading for his living room. I remove my shoes and walk on the impressively polished floor. The apartment feels clad in quality, with a good deal of mahogany and marble deployed around the place. It is a smart, grown-up residence, but sufficiently chewed up and ruined by the kids to feel like home. The height of this apartment affords a good deal of light, and a view of the shuffling gardeners and their rakes outside. We are standing in the middle of the living room, sandwiched between an antique-style fabric sofa and a big flatscreen telly, complete with miscellaneous

consoles and entertainment devices. These reassure me, because Valentine's bookish demeanour might give you the impression it's a house in which Tolstoy is considered light reading and the telly's been consigned to a skip. It's my first clue that perhaps this father of a 'child genius' is more balanced and normal than perhaps he's credited for.

The living room stretches out into a balcony area, with wicker furniture, a coffee table and some toys dotted around.

'So Valentine, what is Ainan's gift?' I ask.

'Well he's the youngest O-level holder in the world for a start,' he says expressly.

'Oh very good. O level in ...?'

'Chemistry. He's presently at a tertiary college, Singapore Polytechnic, doing Chemistry.'

'So he's at university already?'

'Yeah.'

'Extraordinary and he's eight. So that would be ten, eleven years ahead of schedule,' I suggest.

'Yes,' he says. He seems to like this statistic.

'So when did you realise that he had this gift?'

'Well, the thing is we got used to him being surprising from when he was born really. For instance he spoke his first word when he was two weeks old.

I pull a face of incredulity.

'Yeah ... two weeks old,' he repeats.

'What word was that?' I ask.

'Ayer. Ayer is Malay for water. And he would say it whenever he was thirsty. He'd keep on saying it repeatedly until we gave him that, because it's very hot here isn't it?'

Yes it is. Thanks for that.

'So he wanted water,' he goes on. 'But he'd keep on repeating it until we gave him water and then he would stop saying it. And shortly afterwards he started saying poo. Whenever he needed his nappy changing, he'd say poo. So this is a baby who's—'

'Wait wait wait. Stop. Rewind. How old was he when he said poo?' I ask, suspending disbelief for a nanosecond.

'Er, it was just a few weeks later when he started saying poo. He was saying it in context. We knew from the context that it was actually the word, because he would keep on saying that sound which matched a word, until you actually met that sound with the right response for that sound.'

This is white noise now – I'm back in Mr Older's chemistry class.

He goes on, unabashed: 'And when you met that need, he stopped saying the word.'

'And who taught him that word at two weeks?'

'We didn't teach him anything, he just listened. So when he saw water he will have heard the word water. He connected the two.'

'Do you think?' I ask. 'After two weeks?'

'Yes,' he says, without a flicker of doubt in his penetrating, brown eyes.

'Don't you think that's a bit far-fetched?'

'No,' he replies firmly.

Right, OK, I'll go now shall I?

Now in short, I find the baby stuff abject nonsense. I'm lucky enough to have had two children, and when small they made myriad sounds which sometimes sounded like words. But in my view these things are at best coincidence. I can liken it to someone who thinks they've found Jesus's face in the remnants of their tea cup. I respect their right to think they have, but as with all extraordinary, 'miraculous' claims, like conspiracy theories, it strikes me they are there if you want to see them, and not if you don't. It's never an atheist who spots the deity's face in a tree trunk.

Valentine guides me over to the dining table, upon which a copy of *The Guinness Book of Records* is open on the relevant page, offering documentary proof of his son's abilities. Alongside details of Ainan's attainment of a GCSE O-level certificate at the age of seven years and one month is a photo of the boy himself, in a stripy t-shirt, looking surprisingly ungeekish, though I'll reserve judgement on his appearance until I actually meet him. You can rest assured, if I had appeared in *The Guinness Book of Records* aged seven years and one month, my mother would have dug out a shot that didn't look remotely like me – a rare still, featuring brushed, almost ironed hair, a perfect, toothy smile and a momentarily angelic look in my eyes. Every mother has one such shot in her collection. It's usually dragged out the day when you bring your first love interest home.

I was always a big fan of *The Guinness Book of Records* growing up; that and the *Buster* annual were the obligatory contents of my Christmas stocking until about the age of 23. In terms of preparing to meet some of the world's most extraordinary people, it returned to my life as an invaluable resource. That and the trusty internet. Seeing Ainan's face and vital statistics featured in this edition of the iconic publication hit home that Ainan may well have some claim to be a bit of a phenomenon. One of my challenges on this leg of my journey into early cleverness is to establish a sense of how you measure intelligence. Precociously early academic achievements are certainly a valid piece of evidence.

Before Valentine gets the chance to throw more superlatives about his son at me, I suggest we meet the main man. Given that I've been in the house over an hour and he's been somewhere upstairs for the entire time, this already marks him out as a pretty unusual eight year old. We make our way up the stairs, coated in oatmeal sisal carpet, probably the most foolishly stainable colour known to man, and a big no-no for anyone with kids or pets. Tellingly, it's pristine. Don't forget, this is a kid that says 'pooooo' when he needs a shit, so frankly, bring on the light-coloured carpets ...

* * *

We are making our way up to mum and dad's bedroom. As a child, I lived in my parents' bedroom. The smell of Dad's Brut cologne, Mum's talc and a vast bed as soft as a pillow were an alluring combination. They also had massive, heavy velvet curtains that, with a few pulls of the drawstring, transformed the room into a pitch-black darkness. The kind of darkness in which you can no longer see parts of your immediate body. This is not why Ainan is in his parents' room. He's there because in it is a massive bloody computer.

Before we go in, I ask Valentine, 'Are there any dos and don'ts in terms of how to approach Ainan?'

'I would just be friendly but not overbearing.' Valentine clearly has me down as a combination of these two things.

The door swings open.

'Ainan, this is Mark.' Valentine makes this announcement like a courtier would to his king.

I push the door open fully and walk gingerly in. Ainan glances at me for a nanosecond, followed by a blink and you'll miss it smile, before returning his full attention to the computer screen. And let's be clear, he's not watching Spongebob Squarepants. What's on the screen is a dizzying mix of numbers and symbols.

Thus limited to a view of only his profile, it is demonstrably clear what a beautiful child Ainan is. He has large Disney eyes, lips any adult female would die for and eyelashes as long as toothbrushes. Ainan's father is a

Caucasian Englishman, but his mother Syahidah is from Singapore. Valentine would have it that nature hasn't only connived to produce a very pretty child, but one who is one of the cleverest on earth too. A long day at the office for God on that one then. I am not in a position to confirm this yet, and I have a more urgent job at hand. I need Ainan to speak to me.

'Hello Ainan, how you doing?' I say, cheerily.

He looks at me blankly.

'Nice to meet you,' I say.

Nothing happens. I go on, with a game-show host grin, pretending this is going brilliantly, 'So what are you up to?'

Ainan smiles charitably, mumbles something so quiet even he can't hear it, and reverts to the strobing comfort of his computer screen.

It was always a concern on my part, in seeking out children with vast intellects, that I stood the chance of getting a mental kicking from any number of them. I can feel this coming with Ainan. No eight year old is a cinch to talk to when you are a stranger asking annoying questions, but I detected a mightier than usual battle with this little guy. The abrupt body language flagged up the oft-noted correlation of high child intelligence and lesser social skill. It looked like it might be in play here. That, or he took one look at me and thought – twat! It has happened ... But I've learned from dealing with little people (a couple of whom call me dad), that if you have a problem, throw presents at it. Here goes.

'Ainan, I've got a little gift for you.' His head spins round to me on a beat. Bingo. The unassailable law of children and presents has once again prevailed. He is with me now.

'I think you're going to like it,' I say.

I produce a Rubik's cube. A disingenuous gift from me, given that as a child I viewed this object with a mixture of loathing and confusion. For my more laterally minded school friends it was a game. For me it was a pleasant, multi-coloured ornament, to go next to my other favourite ornament: a leatherette-encased Casio scientific calculator. But I felt a Rubik's cube might be up young Ainan's street. Especially this particular model, which appears to have double the squares on it – a supersized Rubik.

'Do you know what that is?' I ask.

'Yes,' he says, dismissively.

A silence follows which is more pregnant than a coachful of women, each of whom is about to go into labour.

'What is it?' I ask, patiently. This is slow work.

'A permutation toy,' he replies.

Incredulous, I ask: 'A permutation ...?'

'Toy,' he says, finishing my sentence.

'A permutation toy, that's one way of putting it,' I say, temporarily dazzled by Ainan's witheringly literal description of this object.

'I'd kind of had it down as a Rubik's cube,' I say.

Valentine pipes up with a smile. His son has drawn blood from idiot boy, and he's loving it.

'His definition is more interesting because it actually says what it is. A Rubik's cube just tells you a brand name. He actually says what it does.'

I concede this point, and pursue the theme with Ainan.

'So do you call hair "product of follicle growth"?' I ask.

Ainan laughs.

Holy crap, I've gone from zero to hero. Though I don't know how many lines of that calibre I have left in the locker to make this encounter bearable. Luckily Valentine picks up the slack and announces that Ainan has, in recent weeks, been practising to take part in a world-breaking memory challenge. Ainan, I'm told, is going to try to smash the world age record for memorising digits of *Pi*. Valentine wants me to be a witness, and to record the official attempt on camera.

After a brief and embarrassing struggle to get the camera *on*, I prepare to film this event as a matter of public record. Ainan is kneeling on the office chair, with his back turned to the computer screen, on which are a perturbingly large number of numbers. Ainan's challenge is to recite as many of these in the correct order, as is humanly possible. Not my definition of true intelligence necessarily, as I understand there are a number of techniques with which to remember vast amounts of data, irrespective of brainpower. But it's still an admirable challenge for an eight year old boy, particularly given that I myself still only have a slender grasp of what my wife's mobile phone number is.

By a lucky twist of fate I've got the camcorder fired up and we're ready to go.

'OK, Ainan,' I say, in an official tone, coming over all Norris McWhirter, 'in a few seconds we will start.'

Ainan is so nonchalant, he looks almost bored at the prospect of this unspeakably vast challenge.

'Are you ready Ainan?' OK. Ready, steady, go.

Ainan then goes on to recite an astonishing series of numbers. All the numbers, which he cannot see, are on the screen behind him, being monitored by dad. I trust Valentine on this. I have to. Ainan just goes on and on and on. After a while there is an abrupt pause. Ainan blinks. Valentine's sphincter tightens. And if I wasn't holding the camera, I'd want the floor to eat me.

Many seconds pass. You could hear a pin drop.

Ainan, staring straight ahead, is calm. He is, at this moment, softly moving his lips, like a child at the nativity play, willing the next line Joseph says to Mary from his mouth. I try not to move a muscle, or make eye contact with Ainan. He is in it – walking the tightrope of his own databank. And I won't be the one at ground level to look up and shout 'yoo-hoo'.

After what feels like an age, Ainan returns from his inert, staring state and suddenly continues with the recital,

continuing as though there had been no interruption at all. It was like a skipping Bee Gees CD, which unexpectedly but mercifully returns to the Gibbs' well-honed harmonies. The numbers come thick and fast, until we reach what seems to be the no-entry bit of Ainan's mind.

'Is that it?' I dare to ask.

'Yeah,' says Ainan, ice cool as ever.

Valentine, eagerly looking at the screen, says to his boy hesitantly, 'I think you've done it, I really think ...'

He peers at the figures in detail. I respect Valentine's hesitation here. The lack of bravado or instant celebration gives me less of a feeling I might be being had. There is a palpable sincerity to Valentine's fatherly pride.

'I think you've done it ... you got up to ... I think you've done fine.'

At this point there is an intimacy between father and son I try to avoid disturbing. I do my best to blend in with the bedroom shutters. They both look at the screen.

'Let's count those now,' says Valentine. '... 518 digits!'

Valentine turns to me.

'That's a double record. It's a world age record and it's a South East Asian record.'

'Incredibly well done,' I say to Ainan. 'Congratulations. Really really well done.'

Ainan has, of course, already moved on.

'Are you quite excited having just broken a record?' I ask.

'Yes,' he says, inertly.

'Great stuff. Is that hard for you to do? Was that a struggle or was that easy?'

'Medium, low challenge,' he says, frankly but not arrogantly.

'Medium, low. Wow,' I say. And memory techniques notwithstanding, it is in my view, a wow.

Valentine interjects. 'If you look at the world ranking list, we've got 518, I think which places us first in the world age rankings. No one of his age or younger has ever done anywhere near that many digits. So if you compare him to all children of his age that places him as number one. If you compare him to all human beings it places him at number seventy.

'Does that suggest that your child who is eight years old ranks probably seventieth on God's earth in terms of power of memory, and that's competing with many clever adults?' I ask.

'Yeah everyone,' he says.

'It's extraordinary, how does that feel for you?' I ask.

'Quite pleased,' he says, about to explode with quite pleasedness. It's a sweet moment. He's genuinely chuffed, and it doesn't look like Ainan has had any fingernails ripped off to achieve this feat. So his remarkable achievement seems to be a win-win on both sides. A fun challenge for Ainan, and tangible proof to the world for dad, that he's right about this kid being something special.

Ironically, even though Ainan is already studying chemistry at degree level part time, he's still legally obliged to go to primary school. Something that dad Valentine is fighting. The next day I went along with Valentine to pick Ainan up from school. I'm not sure if I'm suffering from 'grass is always greener' syndrome, but in my travels I have noticed that all hospitals and all schools abroad seem to be better than British ones. In America, we all know what a dog's dinner their health system is, in terms of access to treatment, but once you've got it – wow. There are hospital wards in America in which I'd happily set up home. I'm sure it's my imagination, but similarly in schools around the world, the ones I've observed have always seemed to have state-of-the-art facilities, inhabited by children who, in terms of manners and appearance, look like an extension of the Von Trapp family.

Ainan's school is no different. Clean modern architecture punctuated with fixtures coated in bright primary colours, with every classroom flanked by a set of windows on either side, affording plenty of light and air. As Valentine and I pass through the corridors, I spot uncrowded classroom after uncrowded classroom, containing expectant, engaged little faces. No chewing gum, no discreetly hidden mobile phones playing Lady Gaga, and no one trying to kill anyone else with a compass. I peer in at one of the rooms, to spot Ainan in the crowd and it is a strange juxtaposition; this child who I yesterday witnessed performing a memory exercise that has propelled him to the elite of global adult memory champions, now relegated to doing an exercise about whether someone should carry their lunch on a tray in the canteen or just in their hands. Ainan doesn't look unhappy, but he does rather cut a figure of an atheist in a church.

Valentine is with me, as we loiter outside Ainan's classroom like a pair of ne'er-do-wells. In spite of the dark blue colour of Valentine's heavy cotton shirt, a couple of large dark wet patches betray the stultifying temperatures the Singaporeans are subjected to around the clock. I like to think if I lived here, I'd have innovated a solution to avoid the sweat patches. All I can imagine is coating myself, daily, top to toe, in Nivea antiperspirant roll on. Which would take about an hour to execute.

I am genuinely impressed by the school: the nuts and bolts, but also the atmosphere. It feels like a happy place. The lunch they eat, steamed rice, fresh vegetables, big bowls of steaming chicken soup, fresh noodles, would make a visit to Nobu look like a downgrade. All washed down with cold water – not a turkey twizzler or can of fizzy pop in sight. But whether it's the right place for Ainan is another question. A question for Valentine.

'Well,' begins Valentine, 'academically, I think that it's almost a waste of his time.' I don't think he means the word 'almost'.

'But when children go to school they learn all sorts of unspoken rules which help them later in life,' I suggest. 'Just aspects of getting on with people you don't particularly like, sharing things, conforming, behaving.'

'Conforming, do you think conforming is a help? I think it's dangerous. Because if you want to be an independent thinker which he is likely to be, you know, a research scientist, you need to not conform. You need to really be able to stand apart and think your own thing. So I think learning a lesson of conformity would be harmful not helpful.'

This is a powerful point, and Valentine is absolutely right to take me up on it. Valentine has lived and breathed this issue since Ainan first said 'poooo'. He does believe his son to be special, a future Einstein or Hawking, and it's true that you wouldn't have wanted either of those icons to have conformed.

Suitably chastened, I go on. 'But doesn't he have the rest of his life in which to develop himself intellectually and to use those talents? What's the rush?'

'If we don't provide the level of education he requires, he's going to switch off. And if he switches off he won't ever switch back on again. And the danger is if you don't make an effort to meet those needs, you will spoil that person's life.'

Valentine is an effective advocate of his son's cause. But it's just one thesis, alongside the state's view which is that every child will go through one system until they are

considerably older. The taxing dilemma is that we won't know who is right until Ainan is a man, by which time it will be too late. It raises the question posed by parents who want to raise their children in a strict faith, or who want to home-school their offspring. To what extent must a parent be right and know best purely because they, by definition, love that child and know him or her best? What role does the state have in protecting these children from the overbearing ideas or philosophy of their parents? A theme I regularly return to in my journeys is balance, something the Singapore state is pushing for by making a child like Ainan attend regular school. But I've noticed that balance is an orthodox, universal virtue more often than not eschewed by the world's most extraordinary people. Particularly those who are unique for their lifestyle choices, balance appears to be the first casualty.

But to what extent can you 'normalise' a child like Ainan? Therein lies the problem with a one-size-fits-all policy on education. Valentine has a job to get the state to cater for Ainan's unique needs, partly because Singapore is a notoriously authoritarian culture, in which obedience is expected of its citizens and in which an act like littering is tantamount to murder. (This is in itself no bad thing – I must confess my inner Richard Littlejohn wouldn't mind seeing people incarcerated for, say, discarding their beverage can from a moving vehicle.) The other challenge Valentine has, for which I can

spy no discernible state support, is to prove how bright Ainan is. By struggling to get Ainan the access to the tools – lab space, books, tuition – with which to expand his knowledge, then Ainan won't have the chance to prove he really is the genius his father claims he is. It's something of a Catch 22, which makes me sympathise with him somewhat.

As I take a break from Valentine's beady glare and take a stroll around the well-manicured grounds, I suddenly have a Columbo moment. Where's mum? I've only heard from Valentine and his monosyllabic, if brilliant, son. This is telling. I think Valentine is intent on delivering a clear message to me about Ainan's abilities and plight. He doesn't want anything muddying the waters; maybe mum is 'off-message' – which, if so, is precisely why I need to meet her. Valentine is a firm advocate of Ainan's academic needs, but I'm here to see the bigger picture – is he happy? Does he play? Does he cry? What's his favourite comic, or chocolate bar? These things – perhaps trivial to the super-intellectual Valentine – are an important part of any child's life. And this journey is about the child, not the parents. I'm willing to hear Valentine out, but I'll know nothing close to the full truth about this boy until I speak to the co-author of his life, his mum. Perhaps she owns the keys to this issue of balance. I hope so – I really hope so. I like Ainan and want to know he has time to muck around, break crockery and stay out too late playing football. I am promised mum is joining us later at the beach. I'm filled with suspense! This notion of a key relative waiting in the wings makes me feel like I'm in an episode of the Jeremy Kyle Show, *Clever Kids Special* ...

The primary school dilemma, and it is one, has been resolved temporarily by Valentine; for now Ainan has a two-tier education. He goes to primary school of a morning, and in the afternoon, while the other kids fool around in their backyard with a tennis ball, Ainan gets into a minibus with dad, and goes off to study at the Singapore Polytechnic. Now it's worth rethinking your prejudices about the word polytechnic, which from a UK perspective conjures images of a sub-university institution, with a campus comprising a couple of sheds, a student bar and an outdoor loo, offering a roster of courses, the most intellectually taxing of which being a Masters in 'Why Jammie Dodgers Are Nice'. This of course was a cruel and unfair perception, but it stuck, which is why in the early '90s the UK polys – the seriously good ones, and the seriously bad – all got called universities. Which is odd, as it's a bit like referring to both the Dorchester, and a tent on a windy hill near a motorway, as hotels.

There are no such branding issues here. Singapore Poly is modern, vast and, like everything in Singapore, utterly pristine. As we walk up the crisp white steps of the building, to the imposing entrance, Ainan looks even more little and young and out of place. Frankly *I* feel too young and little to be here, so God knows how it makes him feel. Through a nexus of corridors and walkways, we reach the Chemistry department. Following the smell of recently exploded sulphur, we wander into one of the labs. It is humming with intellectual activity. Curious faces are crowded around this test tube or that, processing why something has turned blue, orange or red. These faces belong to about six or seven young adults, ranging from late teens to early twenties, and their middle-aged teachers. It's a big, light space, full of bulbs, beakers, tubes, jars, plugs, grips and funnels. The air in the room has a permanent, light haze of cloud, like a stoner's bedroom.

I walk in, apologetically, like a non-drinker walking into a pub. Ainan however strides into the room and seems to know exactly where he is going. Exchanging informal hand greetings with some of his – ten years older – colleagues, Ainan looks like he owns the place. He slips on his white coat and goggles and gets stuck into a seemingly lively debate about some substance that is making that unpredictable journey through a layer of roxyl wool. (Hey look, I said 'roxyl wool' – see, my chemistry education wasn't a complete waste of time.) The forty-something female professor, wearing sensible, *I teach chemistry* shoes, her hair in a strict, unfussy bob, fields answers to the questions this experiment is throwing up. Happily oblivious to my presence, Ainan's hand is up every time, utterly unselfconscious. I suspect he's not showing off; it's rather that he simply knows the answer.

As a mini group, in their white coats and studied silence, they shuffle from one constructed set of tubes and beakers, to another. They finally gather around the obligatory chemistry lab glass cupboard, the glass of which has been dusted by the explosive remnants of years of previous experiments. Valentine and I look on. Ironically we look the most odd; me overly tall and wearing glasses over my glasses (always embarrassing) and Valentine packed into his white coat, and still visibly perspiring. I think Valentine is such an intense guy, he could probably live in the North Pole, and still manage to perspire heavily. But he looks eagerly on as his son sucks in more knowledge.

On paper, I felt there was something inherently dysfunctional about the idea of Ainan going to university at such a young age, and I had a concern that the many ways in which he is already, naturally different, would be exaggerated and indeed made permanent if he enrolled in higher education. But standing in this lab today, getting slightly high from the smell of neat ethanol, it's clear Ainan is, if you'll forgive the chemistry-based pun, in his element. His body language and the look in his eyes scream that this is right for him. It doesn't feel imposed, like so much education feels like for so many. Rather it backs up that this facility caters for Ainan.

But how can I really tell whether he isn't actually struggling here, and everyone is just being incredibly polite? I sidle

up to one of his fellow students, a nineteen-year-old chemistry undergraduate called Chung. I'm very bad at chemistry small talk – 'Hey, Bunsen burners, what are they all about, eh?' – so I cut to the chase and ask him how good Ainan actually is at chemistry.

Chung fires back an instant response: 'Better than us.'

'*Better* than you?' I ask. This is a surprise.

'He is very much better than us,' Chung goes on. 'He knows really a lot more stuff than we do.'

'So how smart would you say he is?' I ask.

'If I'd got an eighth of his brain that would be good.' He smiles, but he doesn't seem to be joking.

'You think you're about an eighth as intelligent as he is?'

'Yeah ...'

Christ on a bike. A further chat with other fellow students and teachers bears out this extraordinary, albeit anecdotal revelation. My straw poll of the room culminates in a sound bite from the avuncular male head of department, a man knocking on the door of sixty, who declares he hasn't 'seen the like of Ainan in all my years'. You have to remind yourself that even taking into account any vested interest this college may have in claiming they house a genius, first of all they'd all have to be liars and good actors. But even if they are exaggerating Ainan's abilities, the bottom line is that he is eight years of age, and unquestionably holding court in this world of adult minds. This episode in the lab, the testimonies, the memory test, the GCSE at seven, calling a Rubik's cube a 'permutation toy', they all point to this child being very special. What muddies the waters is Dad Valentine. Partly because, apparently, he's *special* too. I've been given to understand that Valentine was a child genius himself, but had nothing like the access to the tools for learning that Ainan has, and this is both a sore point and a driving force behind his 'support' for Ainan.

After a lengthy stint at the lab, we head back to Chez Ainan. Valentine serves reassuringly strong tea and a cloyingly sugary take on the custard cream. I take this moment of sweetness to ask a sour question.

'You know, Valentine, some people might observe the situation and think he missed out, he lost opportunities, he's doing it all through the son. He's living it through his son.'

'Not at all,' he fires back, resisting the common politician's refrain of 'I'm glad you asked me that question.'

Politicians never mean it when they say that, but I feel Valentine really is glad I asked that question.

'I've got many things going in my life that's nothing to do with my son. But I'm doing what a father should do, which is to make sure that the son gets what the son needs.'

'But what do you think about people who think you're a pushy parent?' I ask.

'I think that in the context of raising a child prodigy, a true child prodigy there is no such thing as a pushy parent.

There's pushy children. Because the child defines the need, the child defines the territory and you'll find that it's the child demanding of the parent, and pushing the parent forward.'

Beads of sweat appear on Valentine's forehead. He's in fifth gear now.

'For instance Ainan started asking when he was six for chemistry lab access. It took us a year and a half to raise that access. So he's the one making the demand. He's the one pushing for that. He recognises his need, he stated that he wanted this and he's pushing forward for it. It's not us saying "Ainan go into a lab, it'll be fine." It's not that situation. It's not the parent pushing the child. It's the child pushing the parent. And if the parent is pushing the child I would suggest that child is not a prodigy, that child is a stressed-out kid.'

I have to admit that although Valentine may not seem to be the most sympathetic character to meet – he is intense and unnervingly singular about his son – there can be no question he has his son's best interests at heart. The difficulty is in defining what Ainan's best interests are. And wouldn't any 'pushy parent' make a similar set of arguments for why their child needs to put so many hours into a given activity? However, if you meet one parent of a child you only have half the story, so at long last I'm granted an audience with mum Syahidah. Up to this point, she has been an invisible presence – like Arthur Daley's ''er indoors', often referred to, but never actually seen. I'm not too troubled by this because perhaps it's been helpful to encounter Valentine in all his undiluted glory – it's become part of the story. But it's time to hear mum's perspective. My main hope is that she offers the balance Valentine seems to consider trifling.

I take the opportunity of meeting the family en masse, as they take a walk along the beach – mum Syahidah, dad Valentine, his kid brother and Ainan. It's late afternoon, and the wind is blowing like a massive hairdryer over the ocean. It's probably the first time I've experienced the syndrome in which the wind actually makes you hotter. I thought it was a given that this was impossible. Syahidah is extremely beautiful, Ainan having seemingly inherited his fine features from his mother. She has long, thick brown hair, large brown eyes and was clearly a prize catch for Valentine. But she's also warm and serious and, frankly, normal. No speeches about what Ainan said when he was three minutes old. No rants about lab access. This calm, earthy influence she seems to have benefits not only Ainan and his brother, but Valentine too. He is noticeably quieter and less intense in her company. Dare I use the word balance?

Syahidah and I sit down on a ledge, looking out onto the beach. In spite of the soft late-afternoon light, we look out at a less than romantic horizon, dotted with roughly thirty dirty great tankers.

The wind blow-dries Syahidah's already dry hair around her face. I cut to the chase.

'Are you as enthusiastic as Valentine about developing Ainan and pushing him to where he can be?' I ask. 'Or are you a bit more relaxed and laissez faire?'

'Well I think there's more to a kid than just intellectual, there's emotional aspects, there's physical aspect of children and character building so yes, I am not so hot on the academic front. Because there are other issues that the kids need to face up to.'

This isn't just music to my ears. This is Mozart, Mahler and Beethoven rolled into one, to my ears. It's amazing how after a relatively short visit I quickly engage with the characters I meet and have a sense of a stake in their well-being. Maybe that's because, free of baggage and family politics, I'm free to ask the questions others dare not. Here, I'm craving that Ainan doesn't take a path predefined by his father for him. Mum's tone suggests he won't.

'So do you see yourself as a counter-balance in terms of your parenting approach to Valentine, in that you're pushing for social skills and all those other things, and that dad can focus on the academic?' I ask.

'I mean like if it's time to go out, play and he's studying I just take kids.' Hoo, fucking, ray.

'And is that OK? Is that cool with the big man?' I go on to ask.

'I think he was a bit, er, he was a bit taken aback by that. We talked about it and he knows it's necessary to keep

the balance'. She's said it. Unprompted. She's used the B word!

'So what happens if Ainan isn't fulfilled intellectually, what occurs?' I ask.

'He will misbehave in school, he gets bored. You know he lights up if he finds out something and he expands that information – it becomes an idea, he lights up like a light bulb. And although I don't understand much sometimes of the technical aspect what he is saying and then when I see, I think we're doing OK.'

I'm so pleased that mum insists on providing Ainan with as conventional a childhood as possible. Because with a unique mind, a unique appetite for knowledge and a unique father, he's always going to be different. And it's probably right not to fight this. But Ainan's mother is willing to follow a deep maternal instinct that says, yes my child is different, but I'm going to make sure he sometimes gets sand in his shoes, grazes his knees and eats more than his own body weight in ice cream every so often, because he is a kid. And that's what kids do. It is their innate right. It is a crucial part of the journey, and she is right to be the custodian of that.

And she has no doubt had to fight lonely battles against both of her geniuses – the big one and the little one, to enforce some kind of normality, some balance. And of course a break from studying the books to run around the park with

friends is going to lose Ainan some minutes of learning, but it's a price Syahidah understands is worth paying. I'm not sure Valentine understands this, but to his considerable credit, he accepts this, which ultimately is all that matters. And impressively, and perhaps subconsciously, Valentine has chosen a person with whom to have a family and share his life, who counterbalances him. On those rare occasions when a human being gets a relationship right, it's when they are willing to yield to their partner's ideas or wishes, even and especially when you disagree. And hopefully they do the same in return. For example, my wife likes keeping stuff, I like throwing it away – we try to meet each other halfway. Valentine, surprisingly for someone so focussed and uncompromising, has done this. Ainan has and will have an unconventional childhood. But it doesn't come from on high. This family have been bestowed a child that presents his parents with a dilemma.

And you have to put yourself in their shoes – or slippers when they are indoors – and truly imagine what you would do. Notwithstanding the poostuff, what do you do if you happen to bring a child into the world who has a demonstrably unique gift? What happens when you give birth to Mozart, or Einstein or Shakespeare? It's easier said than done. You're damned if you push them, and damned if you don't.

Even mum admits that if Ainan doesn't get access to the tools for learning, it affects his behaviour, and thus his spiritual development. And having immersed myself in Ainan's world, I am less hostile to the idea of him entering an adult academic world. It feels too ideological to hold him back. And somewhat cruel. And for why? If a child is astonishingly good at the piano, do you lock the piano away because the child in question should have a normal childhood first? This encounter has forced me to question why we have these rules about how children should gain knowledge. We are forced to trust that society and the state know best on these matters; never a good idea.

Valentine sweats a lot because he is fighting this. And he's doing it in a place which, by definition, is extremely prescriptive in terms of its citizens. He neither has the financial means – the family is not rich – nor the state on his side. His mission is a story in itself. But as I prepare to go somewhere, anywhere less humid than Singapore, I take great comfort from the various checks and balances that make this family work. For this child of extreme ability, there is a family unit which is quirky, contrasting, a bit funny but ultimately the right one for this particular little prodigy. Tellingly, as we make our goodbyes at the beach, I look over to see Ainan doing what any eight year old would be doing at the seaside. Drawing stuff on the sand with a stick. On closer inspection, it's not a doodle of a smiling face or a space rocket. Ainan is drawing complex equations in the sand. And this is a line in the sand for me. It's the moment when any lingering

concerns about parental coercion in Ainan's case evaporate into the damp Singapore heat.

As I embark upon my final journey, the heels of my Keen sandals worn, my immune system in tatters and my wife barely remembering my name, it's time for one last push. And it will be worth it. My destination is Kathmandu, Nepal. As with Ainan, on this last leg I'm still focussed on little people. But when I say little ...

CHAPTER 5

The World's Smallest Man and Me

PART 1

Small is beautiful

Khagendra Thapa Magar's story

My last journey culminates in perhaps the most extreme and unearthly phenomenon of all. I am going out on a high, looking for the smallest man in the world. As a child, I leafed for hours through a dog-eared copy of *The Guinness Book of Records*, inherited from my brother, complete with a mound of crumbs from a long-forgotten Bakewell Slice. The one part of this treasury of oddity that always caught my eye was the smallest man. These physical phenomena seemed the most exceptional and unusual, in the context of nature's plan. Of course you can find stranger things if you go down the truly freakish route, namely people with three legs, two moustaches or nine eyes. This is a tragic genetic blooper that for me has always been a sad area, unedifying and a general turn-off. Not so with the smallest man. That's because in a sense there's nothing wrong with somebody who happens to be tiny. There is something perfect about them in fact. As I flicked through images of the likes of Nelson De La Rosa, standing at the height of a cricket bat and sadly no longer with us, I was struck by how immaculately formed he appeared to be. From what I've seen in the miniature man arena, everything is perfectly in proportion and therefore not freakish, just a microscopic, abruptly scaled down version of a normal man's body.

An incredibly rare syndrome, it is known as primordial dwarfism and it's a genetic defect that has the doctors baffled. It's not malnutrition, it's not a disease as such and it's not caused by a tumour, as in the case of Sandy Allen and Yao Defen. In fact there's nothing wrong with these men physiologically apart from their tiny size. Their lungs, kidneys, livers, stomachs, eyes and ears are in good working order. The only gripe is with occasional back-related issues, which are a perennial concern for many dwarves too. But these men are not dwarves either. They are a completely unique subset genetically. Your chances of being born like this make your chances of winning the lottery look almost certain. There have been literally a handful of such people through history, and they have naturally always turned heads, with dusty publications featuring photographs of these tiny folk dating back to the Victorian era and beyond.

Khagendra Thapar Magar is a primordial dwarf, and he turned a man called Min's head when he was fourteen years old. Min Baha is a local businessman who lives in Pokhara, Nepal, around two hundred miles west of the capital Khatmandu. A stocky and serious man, he meets me in his appropriately tiny office. Dressed in a navy blue suit, black rollneck jumper and incongruous baseball cap, he sits on one side of his desk, telling me how he met Khagendra. As he tells me, he half gazes out of the window. And it's hard not to. Pokhara is a fantastically buzzing city, with markets everywhere and each bright, dusty street seems to be teeming with teenagers, octogenarians and cows.

A walk anywhere remotely built up delivers a rich kaleidoscope of human activity. There are children playing football with discarded cardboard boxes, there are people standing around yelling about God or the government or both, and there are traders everywhere, plying their particular trade with various degrees of professionalism. And everything here is for sale. It's a massive outdoor version of Wal-Mart, featuring scarves, blankets, homemade soft drinks, books old and new, birds, confectionary, rice, broiled chicken, DVDs and so on. It's all a delight to behold and a far more olfactory and visually alluring shopping experience than a stroll down your average British high street. The only retailers I'm a little unsettled by are the self-appointed and, I suspect, unregulated butchers. If you are brave enough, you can buy a whole array of dead animal, chopped at a table in front of what looks like their living rooms. I can't see a fridge, I can't see soap and I certainly can't see any disinfectant. Now I'm sure this is terrible prejudice on my part, but the homemade nature of these meateries brings out the vegetarian in me, and I'm forced to walk hurriedly by.

Min returns his focus to his office and to me, and explains that he stumbled across Khagendra, hopefully not literally, while visiting a remote mountain village six hours from Pokhara. He's sixteen and is apparently under two and a half feet tall. Min explains that at birth, Khagendra was only six inches long. Yet he didn't see a doctor until he was fourteen years old. And doctors still don't know why he hasn't grown. Min wastes little time in shutting up shop and taking me to meet the man himself. Having relocated to the big smoke, if that's what you can call Pokhara, Khagendra and his parents now live behind the small convenience shop they run.

The road on which they live is like any other in this area, a bumpy, bobbled and dusty track, ground into uneven submission by several decades of heavy trucks and the footsteps of any number of human beings, goats, cows, horses, dogs, cats, rats and the like. This street is the very definition of a thoroughfare, with a cacophony of human activity

ringing in my ears as I arrive. It's the kind of place where a siesta would only be possible with the help of half a bottle of vodka and some hospital-grade sleeping tablets. Outside Khagenda's shop are a team of men dismantling the metal framework of an officially dead truck. Their hammering is deafening and unrelenting.

But it can't distract me from my excitement at meeting Khagendra, a man who may be the smallest gentleman on earth. I'll put up with any amount of hammering to make this encounter happen. The 'shop' is a small opening inside a small terrace of makeshift single-storey properties. There are sacks of rice, barrels of cooking oil and a glass cabinet containing various items, including sweets, tobacco and loo roll. Out front are Khagendra's parents, short, broad and tan-faced. They welcome me warmly. I have to bend down to acknowledge them, as I've grown accustomed to doing since arriving in this country. My various walkabouts, as I'm wont to do when arriving somewhere new, are received with mirth, shrieks of laughter and general wonderment. I feel around twice as tall as your average Nepalese male. I tower over literally everyone as I walk the streets trying, spectacularly unsuccessfully, to blend in. Even the dogs look at me curiously. So it is while imbued with a sense of being something of a freak that I am ushered through to the back of the shop and the living quarters of perhaps Nepal's most physically noteworthy citizen.

I make my way through a narrow corridor into a small living room comprising a narrow bed and not much else. I say not much else, but Khagendra is there. And that's a lot of else. And he is truly extraordinary. It's going to go down as the most physically surreal moment of my life. He appears to have a height similar to that of two teddy bears and has a face about the size of the palm of my hand. He's tiny, far tinier than I could have imagined any sixteen year old could be. Perhaps if I'd had his precise vital statistics prior to meeting him, I might have been better prepared for this massive shock, but I don't think so. I've already seen photos of his cherubic little face and tiny frame on plenty of websites, alongside various theories about his actual size, but no set of measurements can convey just how tiny he really is; you've got to be there. He is dressed in a smart blue trousers and jacket, on top of a little white blouse. The sum of all the fabric involved could scarcely make up a tea towel.

'Hello Khagendra – *Namaste*!' I say, attempting to deploy the local term for 'hello'. 'Nice to meet you. My name is Mark Dolan.'

I bend my frame down as though bending to pick up a leaf off the floor. I pick up something even more tiny and light that that – his hand, which is smaller than my six-month-old baby's hand. Little bigger than a matchbox and surprisingly cold, I shake it, fearing I will break it.

'You are very tall', he says, as interpreted by my fixer Ram. 'Where are you from?'

'I'm from London in England,' I say.

'What is this?' he asks, referring to the large boom pole – a fur-covered microphone that he examines as though it were a piece of wildlife.

'Do you want to touch it? You have to be careful – it bites!' I say, slipping unintentionally into baby talk. I have to keep reminding myself he is a sixteen-year-old man. 'Khagendra, how tall are you?'

His tiny brown eyes, as small as those in a soft toy, are fixated on the various bits of television technology, including the camera. We move to the sofa, where I sit and he stands. He is dancing around jauntily for his assembled audience. He is incredibly cheery and sweet, but his size isn't the only thing that separates him from your average sixteen year old. He has the body of a tiny child, but also seemingly the personality. His attention span is as short as he is, and he seems to respond most readily to the kind of interaction you would normally reserve for a two year old. I expressly didn't want to take this approach, and instead acknowledge that, in spite of his size, he is a young man on the verge of full adulthood. But as he dances around, playing up to the group, it's clear my attempts at any serious questions are somewhat futile.

'Khagendra,' I go on in vain, 'do you find that being with children they don't really understand you as well as an adult does?'

He just smiles and seems to want only to play. He throws his hand in the air, creating the impression of a high five.

'Ah, USA style,' I say. 'That's very good. Give me five! Give me five! Do you know how to give me five? Oh look you're giving me a salute. More military, fair enough. Khagendra, do you know how to give a high five?'

Khagendra attempts to give me a high five, but it seems to be more of a stream of small punches, that an actual high five. It's like being punched by a squirrel.

'Wow – that's quite a significant high five. My goodness I'm being used as a punch bag.' I laugh.

His parents then produce one of his toys, which is a Nepalese variation on an Etch-a-sketch, at which point I lose Khagendra completely. I don't think it's that he doesn't like this strange giant sitting next to him, it's just that he is like a very young child, and seemingly unable to compute some or indeed any of my questions. Once he gets involved with the game, he is oblivious to everything around him.

Among the most extraordinary, jaw-dropping things about Khagendra is his voice. He has the thinnest, lightest voice I've ever heard from any human being. In fact his voice is so high and tiny and squeaky, he makes a new-born baby sound like Brian Blessed. His body is a tiny version of a normal one, but his voice is from another planet. George Lucas could have borrowed Khagendra's voice for one of the peculiar creatures inhabiting his science-fiction universe in *Star Wars*, and

you'd be convinced this was a rare and alien species. As a guitar sounds different depending on its size and shape, so too, it turns out, does the human body, with this miniature man producing a thin, reedy note quite unrecognisable to the human ear. It hammers home what a miraculous rarity Khagendra is.

His father, a warm man and doting presence in Khagendra's life, explains more about his son's development.

'His height has remained the same since he was eleven years old,' he says. His wife sits next to him, dutifully nodding in agreement. 'The doctor has said there is no medicine we can give, as the child is not lacking anything. We have been giving him the same kind of food, balanced diet and different kinds of diet but he's still not growing.'

I'm reassured that they have at least tried to help him get bigger and are clearly willing to relinquish being record breakers for the better interests of their son.

'Khagendra has had no formal education. He started at school, but we took him out, because he was being bullied by other children,' explains Dad. It's a terrible thought; this doll-like child being manhandled by a bunch of ten year olds. It's not a surprise that school didn't work, as Khagendra is so small and fragile, he would barely be safe in the company of a six-month-old baby. Especially if it was a milk-guzzling bruiser like my one. I ask Khagendra's mother, whose South Asian face is beautiful and bears no resemblance to the son

she produced, whether it gets him down, being so small and therefore effectively not able-bodied.

'We haven't found that he's depressed because he is small,' she says. 'And if sometimes people say "you are small",' he says, "No I am big", so he is not sad when called small.'

I wanted to get a sense of how Khagendra is out and about, and what the public reaction to him is, and how he reacts to the public. His parents suggested he needed a new outfit from the tailors, as finding clothes to fit him, that aren't designed for babies, is almost impossible. Obviously I'll be bankrolling this purchase, guessing that as you pay for as much fabric as you use, it's probably not going to break the bank.

We get into the car, his father holding him as we climb in and we set off for Pokhara's answer to Saville Row. I'm sitting in the front and can only hear Khagendra's miniscule, mouselike voice squeaking as he notices random things as we drive along. Occasionally I turn around to look at Khagendra, as he sits on his father's lap. If you were watching a movie that featured Khagendra, you would just assume that he was the work of some of Hollywood's most advanced CGI. But he's not CGI. He's real, and he's sitting on his dad's knee in the back of a people carrier. I'm pinching myself.

Finally, we arrive at a busy marketplace and at the request of dad, we pull up right outside the shop, to limit the amount of public exposure the little guy receives. As with Tom Cruise and Beyonce, Khagendra is such a notable and crowd-inducing individual, he has his own special arrangements when going shopping. They are clearly not overreacting, as the short number of metres it takes us to get from the sliding door of the van to the shop causes about a dozen people to instantly clock the little guy. We get into the shop, and as I turn around, a crowd has already formed at the entrance, peering in at this miraculous human phenomenon. He doesn't know he's a phenomenon though, as he dances around on a raised platform close to the reams of silk and cotton on offer.

'I was wondering if you could help me,' I say to the bearded tailor who greets his celebrity customer with a refreshingly nonchalant air. There are two groups of professionals who are fantastic at this kind of discretion: hairdressers and tailors. Khagendra is made to feel valued and perfectly normal here. There is no fanfare or excitement within the shop, just a quietly professional atmosphere that is focused on giving the customer exactly what he wants.

'I'd like to buy an outfit for this young man. Maybe traditional Nepalese dress please?' I ask, not knowing the first thing about traditional Nepalese dress.

'You want this one? Or this one?' I ask Khagendra. He randomly chooses something white.

'Oh that's, that's a good colour. Or how about this one?' I ask. 'How about red? Let's have a look at red on you ...'

As before, Khagendra's focus doesn't stay in one place long. He spots the crowd and rather than shrink (if that were possible), he begins smiling and waving. He doesn't seem to be doing this for anyone other than himself. It's an unprompted performance and although I feel uneasy about Khagendra's ability to snap into performing monkey mode, I assume this comes from having always had an audience and it may be his way of coping with being stared at. He certainly seems to enjoy it. His eyes are bright and full of life as he darts around, singing, dancing. At one point he pulls out a tiny knife which he brandishes in the air and uses as a prop for his spontaneous performance. I speculate that because of his astonishing size, not only are rosy-cheeked babies a serious threat, but small animals too. I wouldn't fancy Khagendra's chances against a cat or an over-zealous puppy. Thus the small knife is probably a good means of self-defence as well as a performance device.

As Khagendra keeps the show on the road and as the tailor cuts the fabric to within a millimetre, I wander over to the assembled fan club and ask one onlooker what he thinks of Khagendra.

'We heard that he's here, that's why we came to see him. He's very small and he is the dignity of Nepal. We do hope that he'll set up that record as the smallest person. The Nepalese are religious,' he goes on, 'and we believe in God so we think that he is a kind of incarnation from God.'

I'm struck by this wonderful cultural and religious spin on Khagendra's size. I have to think of Vernon Troy, the tiny movie star who is far from deified in our Western culture. Our assumption of the moral high ground when it comes to our attitude to and handling of 'physical freaks' disappears into thin air if you see how his size is played for laughs in the Austin Powers movies.

Given that we are at a tailor's, it's clear that the proximity to a measuring tape is a red rag to a bull where I am concerned. I seize the opportunity to get an assessment of how tall Khagendra actually is. As I roll back a pathetically small amount of tape for the task, I have tangible evidence that I'm not seeing things, or over-egging in my own mind how mini he really is. According to the tape measure of Pokhara's answer to Oswald Boateng, Khagendra is about 25 inches in height, or 64 centimetres. And he's sixteen. It's just amazing. In fact that measurement makes him 8 centimetres smaller than Nelson De La Rosa, the globally famous tiny man who dominates back copies of *Guinness* and whose work is all over YouTube. It seems that Khagendra is in a position to kick his butt in terms of records. But for me, this time with Khagendra isn't about records.

I just want to savour every moment in the company of this chap, as I will never breathe the same air as this kind of human rarity ever again; that you can safely say. And I tend to agree with the bystander with whom I was chatting. There is something spiritual about this chap. His joyful demeanour and supernatural size do create an air of spiritual majesty about him. And he is absurdly likeable. Not only cute and sweet because he is so little, but cute and sweet because of his smile and his blissfully happy eyes. He is incredibly friendly and seems to be a genuinely contented soul. It's unclear how and why someone can be so small but I'm also at a loss to explain how he can be so childlike in terms of his personality. Could it be that after years of being treated as a small child he has fallen into that pattern of behaviour? It's a bit of a chicken and egg question. I suspect it's just the way he is, that as he has failed to grow physically, so he has failed to make the developmental leaps a normal child makes. He can read and count, but to a standard considerably below that of a sixteen year old, and he doesn't seem to have outgrown any of his toys.

During my visit, he seems at his happiest being pushed at high speed on a plastic toy car. Though not how I have hoped the encounter would play out – I have been expecting an in-depth conversation about being a man inside a child's body – I am pleased at least that playing with Khagendra in this way appears to be fun for him and is a way for me to make a connection with him. But as I hold him in the air out back in the family's small, dishevelled yard, it's clear to me I am holding a child in a child's body. A trip later to the local and magnificent Buddhist monastery adds a shade of grey to this assessment. Following another short trip in the people carrier, during which time Khagendra and I bond over a mutual appreciation of my Blackberry, we arrive at the monastery, which is at the top of a steep hill. The mode of transport by which I help Khagendra get to the top is the photo opportunity of all photo opportunities. I must stress that this was Dad's idea and is their solution for getting Khagendra around much of the time: Khagendra is literally placed inside a small carrier bag and carried up the hill. I have the honour, because let's be honest, on a list of a hundred things to do before you die, carrying possibly the smallest man in the world up a hill in a small carrier bag has to be up there.

The bag is tiny itself – Khagendra would be lost in a standard-sized British supermarket carrier bag. As I carry his featherweight frame up the hill, his little head pops out over the edge of the bag, his face beaming with a smile as ever. This encounter doesn't need to get any more surreal, but the man-in-bag moment has pushed it even further into the realms of *holy shit, this is strange*. But Khagendra is happy and in spite of his considerable energies and indeed fitness, he would struggle to make it a quarter of the way up the hill on his own. Like a Jack Russell chasing a rabbit, eventually his tiny legs would give up the fight. As we arrive at the Buddhist temple – a majestic, gold-leaf affair – Khagendra's

playful persona instantly evaporates. As I help him out of his bag (what a sentence!), his face is solemn and sincere. We take off our respective shoes - mine, size eleven Gore Tex Cross-trainers, his a pair of one-year-old baby's moccasins. Looking at them side by side, it's hard to imagine we belong to the same species.

He totters into the temple, which is lined with tens of monks, of various ages, bowing and praying and chanting, in rather fetching dark red robes. He skips around the marble floor, kissing his beads and generally seeming to be elevated by this spiritual exchange. At a certain point, I'm actually struggling to keep up with him as he darts around what is clearly his spiritual habitat. It's a real joy to see how it lifts and comforts this extraordinary little man. He acknowledges the many images and effigies of Buddha around him with a pious bow, before settling down in a corner of the temple to join in the increasingly cacophonous music, banging and chanting. He sits for a good half hour, steeped in thought and emotion.

It's a completely different side to this man and I realise that up till now I'd only witnessed his public persona, something that has emerged as a result of years of being stared at. As we sit in this temple, we inhabit his inner world. It's still a complex issue to ascertain his mental age, as even in private moments with his own parents, he is still remarkably childlike, but this visit to the temple has shown me his soul is a good deal older than his public persona. But even here in the solemnity of this religious environment, Khagendra cannot escape the curiosity his size creates. One of the monks, a muscular young man in his twenties, takes out his mobile phone. The very fact that one of these men has a mobile phone on his person at all is extraordinary, given that last time I checked a monk's robes, there wasn't a pouch for your Nokia. But a mobile *is* produced, and once again Khagendra is prevented by his fellow man from forgetting for even a second that he is different. I remember the lovely tall Ellen in Arizona telling me, on one of our insanely fast drives on the freeway, that she would sometimes look over at someone and wonder why they were staring at her. Eventually the penny would drop – 'Oh yeah, I'm gigantically tall.' That she could forget such a glaringly obvious personal characteristic was a testament to how normal and well adjusted she is. There's little danger of Khagendra ever forgetting that he is about the height of a pedal bin.

I prepare to leave Pokhara, and bid my farewell to perhaps the most incredible example of a human specimen I've ever encountered. And considering my job, that's saying something. I'm in no doubt about Khagendra's physical and emotional welfare, given the close proximity of his parents; a rare thing in these worlds of the extraordinary. His 'manager' Min's motives are a bit more opaque, but I sense that deep down he's a good guy. Min did show me videos of

Khagendra 'performing' at public shows, at which people had paid the equivalent of a couple of quid. From the look of gawping astonishment on their faces, it was clear they were not there to catch his dancing.

I'm persuaded though, that Min isn't in it for a fast buck. I suspect his motivation is a bit of glory in being the man who controls Khagendra's movements. But actions speak louder than words; my dealings with Min didn't focus on the issue of money. There was an agreement I would make a contribution to the charitable foundation created for Khagendra, but no figure was specified, which suggests to me that the baseball cap wearing Min isn't exploiting the wee man. Also the fact that Min has ensured Khagendra's parents are very much part of Khagendra's new, more public life suggests Khagendra's best interests are put first. If you wanted to get rich from Khagedra and wanted total control of this 'human property', the parents would be frozen out. This hasn't happened.

If I am to be critical of the management structure surrounding Khagendra, it's mostly not ethical, even though I am uneasy about the freakshow nature of those public exhibitions. My greater concern is that Min's approach has the whiff of a well-meaning amateur. From my research so far, it looks as though Khagendra, when he turns eighteen, will be declared the smallest man in the world. By some centimetres. At this point there will be a global media stampede in the direction of Pokhara. I'm not sure Khagendra will

be prepared for this, or his parents, or even Min. There is a great danger that this delicate soul will lose his innocent smile and carefree life, once he becomes an international celebrity, and I just wonder how equipped Min will be to make sure Khagendra's life stays as wonderfully normal as it is right now. There's no evidence that Khagendra has any desire to be famous, or to hold this title of smallest man on Earth. I have a yearning hope, as I say goodbye and shake his impossibly little hand one more time, that when it inevitably comes, global fame doesn't change or hurt this tiny, beautiful human being.

As I sit on another airplane and wait for another bag of complimentary nuts to arrive, I just want to rip my seatbelt off, walk down the steps of the plane and spend another few minutes with Khagendra. I have also toyed with the idea of smuggling him in my hand luggage and having him as my best little buddy in my London home for the rest of time. That's how much of a joy he is. As the plane's wheels tuck themselves into the undercarriage of the jet and we tilt upwards towards the clouds, I placate myself by remembering that he is in the right place. For now, at least.

PART 2

The world's smallest man

He Ping Ping's story

But my search for the smallest man in the world offers me no respite. Rather than having a quick pitstop back in the UK, to enjoy a bit of drizzle and some Tunnocks Tea Cakes, I am entreated to fly further east. To Inner Mongolia. As you do. Until I got there, I wasn't sure Inner Mongolia existed as a place, but was rather just a euphemism for somewhere obscure and far away, like Timbuktu. But it does exist, and then some. Inner Mongolia's capital is Hohhot, a pumping, industrialised, capitalised epicentre. The tower blocks here are built so close together the town's planners must have been tied to chairs with mouths gaffer-taped up as these joyless concrete monsters were erected. As we drive closer into town from the airport, there is plenty of architectural evidence of Mongolia's political parentage – the Peoples' Republic of China. Faceless, vast government buildings that are a cross between a factory and a prison, sitting contradictorily alongside huge malls, plastered with neon-lit Western brands.

My stay in this imposing metropolis is to be a short one. I have a night to enjoy the bustle of the city and the considerable luxury of my imposing central hotel. It's one of those

Far Eastern hotels that has about seven restaurants and a chandelier in the hall the size of a small terraced house. On those rare occasions when a good deal has been made with the hoteliers, I try to avail myself of the luxuries available. I'll be the first to put on the fluffy, complimentary white robe and sellophane-wrapped slippers all bearing the monogram of the hotel group. None of the free shampoos, conditioners or body balms will remain unopened. If there is a pool, time rarely allows me a quick dip, but I always pop down, fully clothed, to have a look at what I'm missing. The need for something resembling a full night's sleep supersedes any of the various offerings of these hotels - spas, bars, tennis courts, etc.

There is just one facility I will sacrifice an hour of slumber for, wherever I'm staying. The hotel breakfast. An institution by which great hotels rise and fall, in my humble opinion. The Hohhot breakfast does not disappoint. A smoothie bar, an in-house bakery, a while-you-wait omelette concession, sushi, warm Chinese dishes, the list goes on. And I'm a pig at breakfast, killing the business model of the hotel by returning for more at least three times. The only weak spot is the 'Western style' sausages which are an unnerving offering in hotels throughout the Far East. It's designed to make you feel at home, by offering you bangers for your brekkie, but you'd be better off going native and eating a bowl of eggy noodles. This oriental take on the humble British sausage is a thin,

pale emaciated affair. And the greatest food detective would never get to the bottom of which animal this meaty composite emanates from.

Like an only slightly slimmer version of Monty Python's Mr Creosote, I step into the back of the minibus that will be taking me to the tiny village, inhabited by a tiny man here in Inner Mongolia: He Ping Ping, according to *The Guinness Book of Records* the smallest man in the world. He lives a seven-hour drive from my seven-star hotel paradise. I am to experience the other end of the Inner Mongolian hospitality ladder as I arrive at a hotel near He Ping Ping's place that looks like it was halfway to being built in 1978 and that was where they left it. You know what builders are like – they say they will be back the following Tuesday, and more than three decades later, still no sign. My room, I'm proud to say, is one of the finished ones; it's got windows and a ceiling and everything. It comprises two rooms; a bedroom and, bizarrely, an office area housing a vast desk. It's the kind of desk from which you could rule a third-world country. Given that I am the only customer here today, they've clearly given me the presidential suite. I haven't got long to settle into my abode, as I want to catch the small man before nightfall. I've just got time to have a quick shower, get a change of clothes and order the execution of someone from my massive desk.

I step out of the hotel and onto the street, to inhale the icy air. I'm in Huade City. It's cold here; properly, professionally cold. Holy crap cold. Minus sixteen, to be precise, which occurred to me was colder than the interior of my freezer at home. It's the kind of biting cold that allows you to stay out in it for a matter of minutes at a time. I made a phone call while outside and had to hang up, as after just a few minutes, bones in my face I didn't know I had were beginning to hurt. It's Chinese New Year today and there are splashes of red and gold dotted around this small rural town. The landscape is grey and desiccated, the houses are small stone affairs, with walls about half a metre thick, to keep out the brutal elements. Time is of the essence as my driver, a local, is unsure of the precise location of He Ping Ping's tiny village.

On our way in the van, I pop out and buy a large box of fireworks, a box that could probably house seven or eight He Ping Pings, if the statistics about him online are to be believed. The shop from which I buy them is a small dark general store, as cold inside as it is out. The man behind the counter has a weather-beaten complexion, his cheeks turned beetroot red by the unforgiving winter wind. In fact here, man, woman and child have these characteristic red patches on their faces, demonstrating what a uniquely harsh environment it is in which they live. The man in the general store is warm and genial as he passes me my box of fireworks. That's the wonderful thing about capitalism, even here. A stranger might be frowned upon on the street or in someone's house. But in a shop, a customer is a customer. Just like you are a stranger in a bar, until you've got a drink in your hand; then you are virtually family. This man who is running an independent, Inner Mongolian version of Argos is wearing about five coats and three pairs of gloves and still looks cold. The shop is busy, with dads queuing up for their various goods with which to see in the new year: candles, fireworks, red decorations, sweets, toys for the kids, booze and so on.

I'm very excited to be here at this incredibly important and special time in the Chinese calendar. For many, it's the only time of the year in which people get back to see their wider families, drink some rice wine and get their rocks off. One day off a year; welcome to the realities of the modern Chinese economy. I step out of the dark shop into the blinding light of the mid-afternoon sun. The sun is making scant impact on the temperature, but adds to the sense of Huade City being a very bracing physical environment to be present in. Everybody looks strong and fit. There's very little standing around here, very little chewing the fat and enjoying the moment. I suspect people keep going here, because if they didn't they'd simply freeze in the very spot at which they were standing. I jump back into the bubble of warm air that is my minibus, and finally set off to meet He Ping Ping, the smallest man in the world.

It takes about three-quarters of a minute to drive out of Huade City and into the wilderness. We drive on rocky, frozen roads for a good hour, taking what would appear to be a series of wrong turns. I'm getting nervous. Not only am I hopeful my encounter with He Ping Ping will be successful, but I'm now having to be hopeful it will happen at all. This isn't a part of the world in which Tom Tom or Garmin have any coverage. That particular project will probably stay on their 'to do' list for the next couple of decades.

As the minibus swings around on this rough terrain, bundling me from one side of the interior to another, I'm beginning to feel nauseous. Nauseous and nervous. And no GPS. I'm in a very bad place. I would hop out for some fresh air, but I don't want to step out into an environment which is a good ten degrees colder than the one keeping my fish fingers frozen at home in London. In fact I am informed by my driver who glances at the external temperature gauge on the minibus, that now we've left the urban environment, it's even colder. Minus 20. Wow. Now this is all well and good, but this journey isn't about putting me in cold places to see what happens. That said, I've travelled all this way, thousands of miles, and a cultural epoch away; if I have to do a Ranulf Fiennes and walk the rest of the way to meet this man, so be it. We must get there.

The driver happens upon wind-hardened passers-by every so often, as we near a hamlet here and a village there; the advice of one seems to contradict the advice of the other and we are, I suspect, driving round in circles. My driver, though, with his tenacious air, isn't deflated. He just drives on, with

each road getting rockier and less hospitable than the last. Finally we reach what looks like another hamlet in this spartan landscape. We drive along a narrow road, flanked either side by an unendingly arid backdrop of rolling hills. No vegetation and no wildlife that I can spot. In spite of the insanely low temperature, it seems this place is even too cold for snow.

It's just the dusty, lifeless interior of a butcher's freezer. But astonishingly, somehow, civilisation has emerged here. I count perhaps ten simple stone houses that make up this village. In one of them lives, possibly, the smallest man on the planet. I wander up the pathway of what I believe to be the main man's residence. I am greeted at the door by a rosy-cheeked old lady, broomstick in hand. I gesture that I am looking for He Ping Ping; I demonstrate by lowering my hand to my knee that I am looking for 'the very small man'. There can't be many here. She shakes her head and points me two houses along. I thank her and shuffle to the next house but one, which is identical, but which contains an utterly unique human being. As I glance through the window, I see faces, but none of them look like they belong to a tiny body.

A number of what would appear to be family members emerge from the house, in temperatures that I am informed later are touching minus 25 degrees. They are a handsome bunch, and not tiny. Obviously it's a very special time of the year, so they are all clad in the Inner Mongolian equivalent of their Sunday best. Two guys, both in their early thirties, appear in similarly gelled, jet-black hair, wearing smart, dark trousers, polished black leather shoes and respectively a black leather jacket and a smart navy blue shirt. Just behind them is a young woman, perhaps in her late twenties, glamorously made up and dressed in the kind of evening attire that only works once the sun has set.

'Hi, my name's Mark Dolan and I've come from Great Britain,' I say. I don't know why I've announced my country of origin. I think it's a nervous impulse. Of course in the days of the great Alan Whicker, name-checking either Great Britain or the BBC would put a smile on the majority of foreign faces and facilitate the swinging open of many doors. Not so now, following our recent adventures in the Middle East and our not insignificant contribution to the global meltdown of the banking system. For the record, can I say sorry about those things now? Sorry. Good. I've said it. I hope that helps, in its own little way.

The assembled faces, out here in this bitingly cold wasteland, are pinched and cross-looking, and I don't think it's only down to the low temperature. There is a debate developing between my fixer T and the family members. (T previously drew the short straw escorting me to meet Yao Defen, the tallest woman in the world, who almost pushed her to tears over money.) There is an argument over whether we had agreed to come and whether there would be a payment.

In fact, for weeks prior to our arrival, T had received a series of mixed messages about who controlled access to He Ping Ping, and whether a payment would be made. We had, seemingly, a 'yes' from He Ping Ping's dad, which I'd say is pretty definitive. But curiously, his brother-in-law (the one in the leather jacket) has been claiming on the phone to be He Ping Ping's main representative. Unlike the other chap, who is another brother-in-law (when you are physically unique, it seems you grow brothers in law), this man is aggressive, and I can't help noticing from his breath and yellowing eyes, that he's been on the rice wine a few hours earlier than is customary on these occasions. I plead coldness and we are escorted into the house.

There is an ante-room, consisting of a stove, some food supplies and not much else. We walk through to another room which, it turns out, is the rest of the house; a very small room consisting of a narrow stretch of floor featuring some basic furniture, family photos and a telly. The bulk of the room is a raised platform, covered in plastic tablecloth material upon which, it seems, the residents sit for the majority of the time. The cunning reason behind this is that we are sitting in one of a handful of detached stone cottages in an environment not dissimilar to the North Pole. In fact, amid the barren desolation of the surrounding hills and plains, which are a variety of shades of grey and beige, I feel I've visited the set of a science-fiction movie.

When the apocalypse finally happens, this place won't change much.

And what's extraordinary, is not just that I've wound up in such a dramatic and almost fictional natural environment, but that it houses the smallest man in the world. In fact that it houses anyone is extraordinary. The most dishonest estate agent would find it a stretch to sell this place as a habitat. It's utterly brutal and I find it faintly miraculous that human beings have set up permanent home here and are clearly making it work. Making it work to such an extent that a bead of sweat is actually trickling down my face. The heating system in these houses it incredibly effective. Powered by coal or wood, a boiler sends heat piping through the small property, via a nexus of pipes that lie under the mezzanine platform upon which the family spend their days and, it turns out, nights.

There is a relatively angry exchange between T and 'the brother-in-law'. Either through anger, or inebriation, or both, he has his face pressed against T's as he yells his concerns. I try to step in to help, but not speaking the language and generally being such in incredible outsider as to be a freak, my interventions only inflame the situation. T works her magic and manages to placate him. After much heated debate, an agreement is made to pay this chap four hundred pounds, which should be enough to keep this house heated for the next decade or so. I just hope none of it goes on rice wine or leather jackets. Up till now, the family have kept their prize asset hidden, which, even in this small house, isn't difficult. Now, having agreed this princely sum to meet the little prince, the furrowed brows are replaced with warm smiles. I am hugged by the many and various brothers-in-law present.

In fact there is no knowing how many brothers-in-law I cuddled that afternoon. It might be a world record in itself. The glamorous young woman was in fact He Ping Ping's sister, of which he has two. Also present are mum, a short, wide-ish lady with a similarly wide smile. She greets me warmly with an embrace. Why are almost all mums like that the world over – they're brilliant, aren't they? Dad is sitting on the platform, tucked in the corner, with a long, serious face, a lit cigarette engulfing his forlorn features in a cloud of smoke. He eventually smiles, producing many cracks and fissures in his age-worn face, and waves calmly. Unlike one of his sons-in-law, he doesn't look like the type to get worked up about anything; he comes across as a man who has seen it all before. They are all here, assembled in the room, even a domestic cat – the kind of large house-cat, with fat yellow stripes on his back and bright green eyes, that you could expect to see bossing other smaller neighbouring moggies in your average British garden. It seems this kind of cat is built to survive here too. But where is the main man?

A few seconds pass. Mum tends to a teapot, a sister peels a vegetable. And then, like an apparition, He Ping Ping

appears, literally from behind his father's arm. He walks towards me with a swagger and, incredibly, a fag hanging out of his mouth. He's small, like Khagendra, but he's not cute. And he's *smoking*! All sixty-odd centimetres of him. I have to be honest with you, he is odd-looking. His skin is darkish brown and mottled, and he has the face of a tiny, wizened old man. He is like a scaled-down version of the Labour MP Sir Gerald Kaufman. I know it's an obscure reference, but 'Google Image' him and then He Ping Ping, and you'll see what I mean. It will be worth the interruption to your day, I promise. There is no questioning Sir Gerald's considerable contribution to public life, or any suggestion that the two men are in fact one and the same, but it's a brilliant lookey-likey.

He Ping Ping, not Sir Gerald, walks towards me, and I'm frankly a bit scared. Scared, of the smallest man in the world – imagine! He just has a faintly sinister air, like a diminutive Bond villain. He keeps the cigarette in his small mouth as he comes over to shake my hand. He is of course tiny, but that's not what is preoccupying me at this moment; it's rather his unfriendly manner. He is a cool customer, eyeing me suspiciously with his wide, blinking eyes. He has an air of arrogance that I wasn't expecting. And I ask myself why I wasn't expecting that. Your size or any aspect of your appearance should never be expected to define your character. But I am perturbed none the same. I certainly don't feel like he wants me to be there.

I take my shoes off and mount the centrally heated platform. So effective is the heating in this house, I actually peel off a layer and get myself comfortable. I start off by asking He Ping Ping what I hope will be some nice easy, entry-level questions.

'What things do you like doing?' I ask.

'I like poker and I like driving,' he says without, at any point during his answer, making eye contact.

'Driving. What do you drive?'

'Yeah, I've been driving; I drove a four-wheel drive.'

Looking at his size, he's a little taller that Khagendra, but not by much. So how he managed to commandeer a four-wheel drive vehicle I'm not sure. Even I feel small in one of those. But it sends a clear message - He Ping Ping wants the world to see that he is a nineteen-year-old man, with a nineteen-year-old man's interests and that just because of his size he isn't any kind of baby. Of course that is completely right and understandable; it's just that my last encounter with Khagendra had forced me to treat him as a child to connect with him. Now I have to make sure I go back to the plan that I started with at the beginning of my journey into the world of small men: to put to the back of my mind his size and drill it into my psyche that this is a man. The conversation moves to the world record; I wonder how featuring in *The Guinness Book of Records* might play to his bravado.

'How would you feel if you discovered that you were the smallest man in the world?' I ask.

'In my heart I wouldn't like it,' he says, with pathos.

'Why wouldn't you be happy if you were the smallest man in the world?' I ask, pushing the point.

'I am just not happy about it,' he says, turning his back to me symbolically and lighting another cigarette. A cigarette which is the best part of three times the length of one of his fingers. We aren't hitting it off and I feel that he just doesn't want to talk about his size. It doesn't help that I don't smoke. I think if I was able to share my stash of Marlboro or Camels with him, there would be an opportunity for some kind of connection. It seems his entire persona is built around contradicting and even denying his physical size. With my questions drawing attention back to his size and my own sprawling height accentuating the differences between us, the encounter is not going well.

He is answering my questions, but he doesn't like me being there and he doesn't like the cut of my jib. What pains me is that it pains *him* that I am asking these things. The last thing I want from any of my meetings with these unique and often vulnerable people is for there to be any sense of this being a painful experience. If it is, then it defeats the object. I'm not here to be Jeremy Paxman to his Michael Howard. These encounters, though at my behest, need to be a shared experience and a voluntary one. In fact if the person I meet is having fun in my company and perhaps enjoying a right to reply, I feel I'm doing my job properly. Here at this very moment in

time, I am all out to sea. I feel like a newspaper hack must feel when they've doorstepped someone's wife to ask her about the sexual shenanigans of her footballer husband.

If He Ping Ping was in Birmingham, or any other place reasonably near home, I'd be tempted to say, 'OK, look, you're not comfortable – let's call this a day.' But he's not in Birmingham. He's in Inner Mongolia's frozen Tundra. I will never be here again. I cannot walk away now. I decide to rapidly revise precisely what my motives are. And they are what they always were. To hear the story of somebody so unique. To look behind the photos and video clips on YouTube, and to meet the real person. Having reassured myself that that's the only reason I am here, I decide to give it one last go.

'Would you like to be famous?' I ask.

'No, I'm not happy – you're happy. I'm not happy,' he says. I am shocked by his answer. And sympathetic. There is real pathos about this man, even if I'm partly to blame for unearthing it.

'Do you know why you are so small?' I ask.

'Er ... I don't know,' he says, walking over to his brother-in-law and 'manager' and acquiring another cigarette. This must be his fifth in the short few minutes we've been together. He is a chain smoker.

We take five. I retreat to a corner of the raised platform and sit gazing out of the window, towards the dusty, icy noth-

ingness. And thinking I've got nothing from this encounter, only an unhappy interviewee. It's Frost–Nixon all over again, and this Frost is having a mare. He Ping Ping continues to smoke with his family members and plays with the tom cat, which is something to behold. He Ping Ping lifts the cat in the air and plonks it on his tiny lap.

The cat looks vast next to him; their faces are a similar size and the cat is considerably longer, stretched out. He plays roughly with the cat, slapping it and pulling its tail, which in terms of physical scale would be like me hopping into the lions' enclosure of Edinburgh Zoo and having a tussle with one of the big cats. This cat, though, defers to He Ping Ping. The human being still remains higher up the food chain than the cat, in spite of the size discrepancy. After a few minutes during which I sip Chinese tea and generally try to be invisible, I return my attentions to He Ping Ping. I try to strike a conciliatory note.

'He Ping Ping. I'm very sorry if I asked you questions you didn't like,' I say.

'Thank you,' he says, glumly and still not making eye contact.

'You don't like those questions do you?' I say.

'Yeah, I didn't like the questions. I don't like you,' he says. My heart sinks even lower, to the pit of my stomach. I'm getting a kicking from the smallest man in the world.

'Do you really not like me – or is it just my questions?' I ask.

'I just don't like him,' he says to my interpreter T, but referring to me. 'I just don't like his head,' he explains.

I take my annoying questions and my terrible head, and get his brother-in-law's advice on this. I didn't think, when I met this man outside an hour ago in the freezing cold that I'd so quickly be turning to him for help. While He Ping Ping gets enveloped in preparations for the big party in the evening, I take the brother-in-law aside, and ask him where I'm going wrong.

'I guess it's because like everybody else, you don't want to talk about your shortcomings', he says with surprising candour and insight. 'We don't want to talk about the fact that we are different from other people, so he would rather just play and not think about it and avoid the questions. I think that's why he's like that.'

'Is he often like this?'

'He's quite temperamental and he has a quick temper,' he says.

Mum chips in, while polishing a kitchen utensil, 'When he's not happy he will throw his temper tantrums – he'll throw things, he'll refuse to eat. Everyone kind of spoils him at home so he gets away with it.'

OK, so I feel that while I could have played all of this considerably better, it's not a lost cause, and perhaps I can comfort myself with the knowledge that he can be prickly by

nature. It's a challenge to win him around. I leave the subject of size to one side and instead quiz him about his smoking, which is a perpetually surreal thing to witness.

'He Ping Ping, how many cigarettes do you smoke a day?' I ask.

'Two packs a day,' he says nonchalantly.

I am astonished. I physically couldn't get through that many cigarettes, even if I practised. And my lungs must be five times bigger than his. It's a tragedy to watch this otherwise healthy man, who is smaller than a toddler, poisoning his tiny, miraculous body like this, with every puff. It all started, his mother tells me with a sad countenance, when he was younger. Tradesmen from other towns would come and give him cigarettes, as they found it funny to see a chap of this size puffing away on a fag. I think there's no doubting the veracity of this story, though the adult and masculine nature of smoking is clearly attractive to He Ping Ping. The fags feel like more than just the work of some pranksters from out of town. They are a prop, a symbol of being a man and being big and being normal, things He Ping Ping craves and which were denied him because of a crucial missing chromosome or genetic kink.

Something I've been putting off and which I fear is going to kill this meeting stone dead altogether is the issue of He Ping Ping's precise height. Though not as definitive as the official *Guinness* procedure, I cannot come all this way and

not ascertain with my own tape measure just how tall he actually is. I decide to bite the bullet and ask him straight. I wait until he gets his next cigarette lit by his own father before popping the question.

'Would it be OK if I measured you?' I ask, to the point.

'Let me measure you first,' he says, unexpectedly playfully. 'I'm going to measure you now,' he goes on.

He grabs the tape measure and gets me to lie down fully. He clambers over my body, dripping ash as he moves around. He seems to be enjoying this position of superiority and control as he stands over my defenceless frame. He darts from one end of my unending body to the other. He is smiling and gesturing to his amused familial audience. Perhaps I needed to let my guard down in this way for He Ping Ping to accept me. I have to give way and let him be boss.

'Three and a half metres, no four metres,' he declares, inexplicably. He's even worse with a measuring tape than I am.

'Eleven foot one,' I say, making a rough calculation. 'Sounds about right,' I remark, trying to capitalise on the mood of frivolity and fun which has emerged here. I feel that handing over control of the tape measure and my entire body has produced a turning point in my relations with He Ping Ping, to the point where the only tricky thing about measuring *him* is not getting my hair singed if I get too near his burning cigarette. That would be something: given a mental kicking by the smallest man in the world and then torched by the self-same man.

'I'd say you are around seventy-four centimetres in height,' I tell He Ping Ping.

'I should be seventy-three centimetres tall,' he retorts. I don't argue with him; I'm conscious my method is vague, and I don't want to disrupt our fragile peace.

To sustain the momentum of all of this unexpected warmth, I figure now would be a good time to hand over the gift of a huge box of fireworks. He Ping Ping, who has now settled over in the corner with his cat, his brother-in-law and his latest cigarette (I'm honestly not exaggerating!) spots the box and springs to his feet and bounds over. He is thrilled and as the sun has set on the day, I'm pleased at how things are playing out. Earlier I might have expected him to shrug and walk away at being offered such a gift. Now, with defences down and everyone's sincere and harmless motives on the table, the gift is received with joy and excitement. It's also a reminder that gifts are a rare thing in He Ping Ping's life. He may be rather famous, but for the entirety of my stay there, I don't see a single luxury item belonging to the little man. Just his prized smokes. But in Inner Mongolia, cigarettes come nearly as cheaply as puffing on the air itself, so they don't really count.

'Can I lift such a heavy thing?' he asks as he tries to get his toy soldier arms around the box. It's wider and taller than he

is, but being crazily determined and energetic, he manages to get some purchase on it. If this was a movie, shot to scale, it would look like a normal-sized man carrying a red telephone box. Unperturbed, He Ping Ping drags it to a handy spot on the platform and gives it a detailed inspection.

'This is a very nice gift,' he says, tenderly. I'm beginning to realise that the initial caustic reception I received from the main man was typical of any celebrity being weary of being pestered and asked the same stupid questions over and over again. Now that he's made his point, and made me treat him normally, man to man, I am allowed into his world.

I get comfortable on the platform again, and I'm curious to know what this lovely cat is called. I ask He Ping Ping, who seems to be its master.

'Cat. Just cat,' he replies tersely. No sentimentalism here, in minus 25 degree temperatures. It's about not freezing or starving; it's not an environment where people are prone to sitting around and having lengthy discussions about what to call the pets. As he embarks on another unedifying fight with this moggy, He Ping Ping quietly mutters something that, once T has translated it properly for me, warms my heart.

'Hey, tonight, eat with me,' he says.

'OK. I'd love to,' I say, genuinely touched. He Ping Ping has done an amazing about-turn, and I feel honoured to have, to a certain extent, won him over. I'm not sure how or why it's happened, but it's made the whole trip worthwhile. It's New Year's Eve, and the Inner Mongolian equivalent of Morecambe and Wise are on the telly, there are the remains of a pig bubbling in a pot in front of us, and I'm feeling celebratory. I'm here with this amazing young man and his family, on a day they wait a whole year for, and I am sharing the experience. It's a privilege.

'Cheers,' says He Ping Ping to me, brandishing the orange squash we're both drinking. He might put away two packs of cigarettes a day, but at least he doesn't drink.

'Yes, cheers,' I say, clinking glasses with the smallest man on Earth, well until Khagendra turns eighteen anyway ...

'Look at mine, look at mine – I'm going to drink it all,' he says animatedly. He sinks some, but not all of it. Watching him eat, with his tiny hands, shovelling food and drink into his tiny mouth, further accentuates just how small he is. I'm mystified as to where the food actually goes.

'Welcome,' he goes on, in a raised voice. 'Welcome to Inner Mongolia. Welcome to our home.'

'Well thank you, it's a joy to be here,' I say, still astonished at having shed my persona non grata status.

'Don't be shy,' says He Ping Ping, referring to the pig in front of us.

Watching dad slicing up a set of incredibly fatty chunks of pork, I'd been hoping I could get away with a bowl of rice. Not so; I had a veritable audience before me, watch-

ing me masticate every chunk. It was my 'I'm A Celebrity' moment, and I was reminded, as I swallowed whole lumps of grizzle, why I would never appear on such a show. But with everyone's mood having lightened, and with this dish being a speciality for new year, I wasn't going to spurn the family's hospitality.

After a couple of hours of eating, drinking and chatting it was time to head outside to light the fireworks I'd purchased from the Hohhot branch of Argos. I'm not big on fireworks. I've always thought there are so many ways that young people can accidentally become injured in life, that we don't need to have a special day every year to almost guarantee that will happen to some unfortunate person. It's the health and safety officer in me that baulks at the sight of a well-meaning but over-zealous dad running from a small burning rocket as it sits precariously in an empty plastic Coke bottle. It's just not my thing, and it fills me with terror. I realise I'm on my own on this one. I certainly am in this household, where they watch in collective awe the various fireworks on show. Enjoying it most of all is He Ping Ping. To give him a better view, I pick him up. Again the idea of picking up a man and holding him in the air is incredibly strange. As the illuminations light his face, reflecting little pools of fire in his eyes, he is like a deity, as Khagendra was. An unearthly phenomenon and a reminder of the miracle of nature.

'Do you want to get down now?' I ask. He nods, and then scurries over to a recently burnt-out firework at the end of the yard.

'Careful, no, no no!' I shout. 'Stop! Stop! Stop! Stop! Stop! Stop! Stop! Don't Touch it! No! No! No!' Shouting now, I say, *'He Ping Ping, come away!'*

Finally he retreats from the smoking embers of the last firework and begins jogging back to me. My heart is still in my mouth, having thought I was about to watch the smallest man in the world go up with one of the rockets. I wasn't sure whether my innate sense of protectiveness came from the fact that he is small and therefore so vulnerable, or whether this miniature human being had become, in the course of a rollercoaster day, my friend. I like to think the latter. Like Khagendra, he too is an extraordinary person. His physical size is only part of the story. Though a more spiky and egocentric character than Khagendra, and most definitely more blokey, He Ping Ping still possesses that elusive, almost supernatural magic unique to these Lilliputian figures. I remember being captivated by the story of Tom Thumb as a child, and I feel that in Inner Mongolia and Nepal, I have come close to stepping inside that fairytale.

For all of the extraordinariness all human beings have to offer, whether physical or mental, nothing will rival the experience of shaking the tiny hands of these remarkable men. Suffering the ultimate setback on the path to manhood, these two chaps have a strength and an honour lacking in so many people four or five times their height. They've been handed a duff card by nature, and notwithstanding annoying men in glasses asking annoying questions about what it's like to be so small, generally they both seem to manage life extremely well. They both possess a strong will, huge charm (when they want to) and seemingly limitless energy. Far from hiding behind the nearest inanimate object (and given their size, they are spoilt for choice), they prefer to grab life with both hands and be the centre of attention. The fortitude of spirit and crazy courage they demonstrate, in the face of the greatest kind of physical obstacle, is both humbling and inspiring.

The intoxicating irony of these encounters is that ,as I walk away, and head back to a part of the world which has normal temperatures, I genuinely feel I have been in the company of a pair of giant men.

EPILOGUE

Hairy Larry and Cat Man Dennis

Two sides of the same extraordinary coin

As I reach the closing stages of my journeys into the extraordinary, I am struck by the stories of two men who sum up both ends of the spectrum of human oddity. Larry and Dennis. Larry, like Khagendra, He Ping Ping, Sandy Allen and others, was born unique. Like them, large aspects of Larry's life were predetermined from the moment his parents (hopefully) passionately conceived him. The majority of us are in the privileged position of at least having the illusion of autonomy in terms of how life plays out for us. Yes there are factors beyond our control: genes, parental influence and, to quote Harold Macmillan, 'events dear boy, events'. But to be born with ninety-eight per cent of your body covered in rich, deep, dark curly hair rather pulls the carpet of fate from under your feet. Born in the Mexican town of Loreto, Larry

Gomez comes from a family for whom incredible hairiness is passed down in the way high foreheads were in mine. Luckily I've got a fringe to hide mine, but there's no disguising, hiding, shaving or lasering Larry's hair. It's here to stay. But this is not a sad story. The family love their hairiness. It's a badge of honour, a symbol of virility and it's a coat of membership to a family whose hairiness dates back several generations.

Larry may have had his appearance decided for him by a hairy great grandfather all those decades ago, but as I stand in his Californian garden in late 2008, sipping one of his ice-cold beers, I meet a man who is absolutely in control of his destiny. Larry is no victim. Standing at around 5 ft 10 in in height, slim, muscular and sporting a pale brown Levis t-shirt and jeans, he appears to be anything but a victim. Speaking in a mellifluous Spanish-American accent, his thick bristles protect him as we stand in the sun; I, meanwhile, am burning up. His face, a full, dense foliage of hair, is strangely handsome. The mane starts at the top of his head, covers his entire face and continues down his neck towards his chest. The facial coat is faintly regal. If an alien came down to Earth, met Larry, then me, it would most likely assume I was the freak of nature. His eyes, like two large brownish diamonds, shimmer in the undergrowth of curls. I'm no expert in these matters, but I'd say he's 'cute'. His lips, which are free of hair, are sensuous. Surrounded by a bushy fleece, they create the illusion that he is always pouting slightly. Adding to his allure are a set of unendingly long, curly eyelashes Greta Garbo or Lauren Bacall would have killed for.

But Larry is a real guy. A survivor. He's not in show business, any more. Circus sideshows are still all the rage in Mexico, where Larry could easily be enjoying regular work by swinging from a trapeze, balancing on a unicycle or just parading himself around in a suit, stared at by stunned audiences. Unlike some of his relatives, he has rejected that. His body is not a meal ticket any more; too high a price was paid for selling a fictional version of himself i.e. 'wolfman', 'the human ape', etc. Larry, like so many of the people I have met on these journeys, craves normality. He wants to be a regular Joe; to put a roof over his head, put gas in his pick-up truck and put food on the table and maybe a couple of Coors Lights in the refrigerator.

The condition that makes Larry the way he is, is called hypotrichosis, essentially a syndrome of hyperactive hair growth, manifest across a vast amount of the body. When I called the men in white coats to ask how I can tell if Larry is the world's hairiest, they told me not to bother. We are all, in fact, covered completely in hair. It's just that our hairs that can't be seen are light and tiny. So whether Larry is the hairiest is a matter of cosmetic judgement. If you glance at a photo of Larry, featured in this book, you will notice that he is indeed utterly, compellingly unique. In fact children have

been known to cry on seeing a photo of Larry. (That said, there are some pictures of me aged seventeen on a beach holiday wearing my short shorts that would provoke a similar reaction.) He is certainly hairier that any human being I have come across in person, in print or online. Indeed he is something of a celebrity, having featured in magazine articles and appeared on TV shows, along with his hirsute cousin Chuy. Ironically, Chuy is still in the circus, but in America, where because of political correctness, he's only allowed to do backstage work, like operating the curtains and installing the tent when it arrives at a new town. It's a strange twist of fate; it's a bit like getting Sir Steven Redgrave to varnish a canoe.

Larry has walked away. Walked away from the circus, and walked away from the body he was born with. He has made a new life in San Bernadino, a neighbouring offshoot of Los Angeles. He rents a small house which boasts the obligatory front porch, and a small rear garden, littered with car parts: engines, gearboxes, carburettors. Larry is a man's man. And he has a man's man's job: he's in construction, specialising in roofing. What I was struck by is how normal his life is. He has clearly shrugged off the hairs, metaphorically, and joined the rest of society in trying to get by. He is completely accepted when he walks on a building site (not something I'd ever be able to boast) and is a popular figure in his local neighbourhood. When we take a stroll to the local Mexican fast food joint, he flirts manfully with the young waitress;

she giggles at all his jokes and her body language is most forthcoming.

So Larry's story is one of self-acceptance. *Yes, I'm hairy – now let's move on*. If you make a career from your physical characteristics, then move on you cannot. Larry jumped off the gravy train and made himself a citizen of the real world; no mean feat if you consider how hard it is to shake off the endless stares and unwanted attention. But he has done it. He wears his appearance with ease. There's plenty of hair on his shoulders, but no chip. This fortitude of spirit hasn't come overnight. Larry was in and out of show business for years, and finally decided to recover his soul, before it was gone completely. One of the big surprises about Larry was just how popular he is with the ladies. He talks me through the string of girls he has courted in his life and even shows me photographs of the stunning young woman who was once his wife. Sadly that marriage didn't work out, and Larry has scant access to the little boy (hairless, I might add) the marriage produced. Larry's determination to make money and eventually make a home for his boy draws in to sharp focus the true priorities of life. If that's what's important to Larry, who has had a hard life – would you or I like to be born that way? – then the message is clear. It's all the basic things that matter. Love, keeping a roof over your head, and having the occasional cold beer in the garden with your friends. I have every best wish for Larry and his future, that will hopefully include his beautiful little boy.

This is in stark contrast with Dennis Avner. AKA 'cat man', or 'stalking cat'. He was born 'normal'. But over the last two decades he has undergone a series of operations to turn himself into a jungle cat. A drive from LA through Death Valley takes me to the one-horse town of Tonopah in Nevada, home to a man who has made himself extraordinary. He lives in the worst house on a great street. Amid the smart, white timber houses stands a dishevelled and unkempt trailer – welcome to Chez Stalking Cat. I ring the doorbell and open swings the door. I am presented with the overwhelmingly intimidating sight of a large, wide man whose face is completely covered in stripes, wearing cat's eyes contact lenses, studs in his cheeks (for whiskers, don't you know) and a set of fangs where his teeth used to be. I've seen photos of course, but nothing prepares you for meeting this cat in the flesh. His voice is strangely deep and booming, even for a big man, and I have the surreal feeling that lovely Sandy Allen has metamorphosed into this feline creature. And given Sandy's desire for a little 'kitty cat', she'd love Dennis's place. I'm not sure she'd want to pet him, as he is genuinely scary looking, but the whole house is a monument to all things feline. There are literally hundreds of cat photographs and paintings on the walls and littered around the place. And Dennis isn't the only cat living there – he has a couple of real cats to keep him company.

If I am to be honest, his home is horrifying, like one of the murder scenes from the film *Seven*, just without the corpse. The smell is rank, the carpets are sticky and covered in fur and the place is in almost total darkness as all the moth-eaten curtains are drawn. A visit to the bathroom is an experience that will stay with me forever – let's just say the cats pretty much have the run of it now. Any human being hoping to take a leak in there should get every jab going before doing so. This is not to mock Dennis, but rather to illustrate what an unhappy bunny, sorry kitty, he is. It turns out that Dennis is another of life's survivors; a perennial theme of my journies. As we sit down in the least dank and filthy part of his living room, we plan our impending voyage together. In the unlikeliest buddy movie of the century, Cat Man and I are taking a road trip to Las Vegas. He is house hunting, with an eye to a permanent move to Sin City. It's on that trip that it becomes clear that Dennis's journey in life mirrors that of Larry, but in the opposite direction. Dennis explains that his decision to cloak himself permanently in feline paraphernalia, with the help of a body artist, was his way of being himself, of coming out, of shedding the lie of his previous 'normal' self and of fulfilling his destiny.

A happy road trip ensued, with the two of us discovering a shared passion for the works of Steve Miller, The Stones, Elton John and The Who. A charmingly high-maintenance diva, catering for Cat Man's various needs – his smokes, soft

drinks, snacks and his beloved buffets – made the likes of J-Lo and Mariah Carey look positively self-sufficient. Noticeably fat, and sporting the largest man breasts I've ever seen, Dennis eats more like a Rottweiler than a pussy cat. On arrival in Vegas, the buffet that he has spent the last nine hours talking about has just closed. It's only 8 p.m. and the chef's gone home – it's back to the American madness of early dinners. Arriving as the waitresses mopped the floors and upturned stools, Cat Man was disconsolate. We tried to make amends by taking him to a normal restaurant – not a buffet, much to his chagrin – where he proceeded to devour what I'd estimate was a quarter of a cow. His verdict after ingesting his last morsel of meat? 'Not bad, but not as good as a buffet.'

It's cheering though, that Cat Man is so bolshy. Too many of my subjects in these journeys are victims. Now that Cat Man has reached the surgical tipping point of being more cat than man, there is an assuredness, a wild confidence that makes him supremely secure. He's now a cat and so, like his real feline cousins, he doesn't give a fuck about the human race. It goes without saying that the road trip, in between cigarette breaks and lengthy discussions about which buffet was the best in Vegas, threw up a harrowing portrait of the kind of childhood Cat Man had. In short, Dennis's early years make Dave Peltzer's sound positively idyllic. It's heartbreaking to hear what Dennis says he went through and is therefore understandable why he chose to become someone else. So inculcated in self-loathing, he not only became another person, but another species.

After school, Dennis joined the US Navy as an engineer, after a few years of which, he dropped out and became a professional drinker and drug user. After a couple of decades of full-time self-destruction, he met a body artist who suggested he could help Dennis fulfil his lifelong dream of becoming a big cat. Dennis contends that it was this chink of hope that gave him the strength to dust himself down and quit his booze and drugs hell. The proof of the pudding is that now, in his mid fifties, he is here, clean and relatively sober. I am struck by an eerie parallel with Sheyla Hershey in Brazil, the woman who told me 'these boobs saved my life'. So the whiskers, the tattoos, the four-inch fingernails, the raised upper lip, the silicone in the cheeks and the fangs have all perhaps coalesced to save this ex-man. But he has paid the price; he has been rendered almost penniless because of all of the procedures, he has experienced an incalculable amount of pain as most of the work was done without any kind of anaesthetic and it's almost impossible for him to ever again have what might be termed a normal life.

The good news though, as he insists to me in his already stinky Vegas hotel bedroom, is that he doesn't want a normal life. Call him a freak if you want, and perhaps that is what he has knowingly made himself, but that was his journey, the one he chose to make. Larry just wants to go to the shops and buy a loaf of bread, Dennis wants to be photographed on Sunset Strip with his fangs out. One gave up being a walking circus sideshow, the other paid good money to become it. But either way, both men are happier, better adjusted and more well now than before. And this, I try to learn from. These two amazing human beings are both titans of destiny in boldly dramatic and different ways. Their lives, like ours, have been an untidy work in progress. But progress just the same. They have achieved the greatest goal to which everyone knowingly or unknowingly aspires, that today is better than yesterday. And tomorrow will be better still. It's what gets me and you out of bed in the morning, and Larry and Cat Man and the wonderful cast of characters I've met on these journeys. If we are not on a journey, and following our own crazy route, we are not really alive, and far more pitiable than Sandy, Khagendra and Minka put together.

I miss all the people I've met. Variously kind, clever, generous, elusive, cranky, unpredictable, crazy, but never ever dull. I especially miss, though, two fabulous human beings who have tragically passed away since the writing of this book. The remarkable and formidable He Ping Ping sadly passed away recently aged 21. And the beautiful, majestic Sandy Allen has also died at the age of 53. I found out later from Jane and Linda that Sandy had asked to be buried with, amongst other things, the necklace I'd bought her on our shopping trip together. He Ping Ping and Sandy Allen, you both did it your way; thanks for letting us share briefly your extraordinary lives; we love you and we miss you.

All the people I've met either put their head above the parapet or had nature do it for them. To witness the courage and strength of will that has been required to make every step on their paths in life, has been a true inspiration. These people are all miraculous, not because of what has happened to them in life, but how they reacted. They all want the same thing: to be normal. But *their* kind of normal, not society's. These human beings have made me realise that we all need to work out what normal is for *us*, and then spend the rest of our time on this mortal coil, working to get there.

ACKNOWLEDGEMENTS

To describe this whole endeavour as a team effort would be a colossal understatement. The TV series itself was the end product of the ingenuity, hard work, commitment and creativity of the following people: Tanya Freedman, Alicia Kerr, Krishnendu Majumdar, Kate Townsend, Guy Gilbert, James Bluemel, Krishna Govender, Kirsty Cunningham, Norman Hull, Kathryn Tregidgo, Danni Davis, Sheena Cameron, Emma Shaw, Charlotte Rodrigues, Holly Davies, Simon Howley and Alex Sutherland. Also the marvellous Vik Sharma, Lynda Featherstone, Tee Tsay, Anna Price and Will Grayburn. Tanya, Krishnendu and many others in the production team took and provided many of the photographs that feature in this book – many thanks.

I'd also like to sincerely thank Alistair Pegg, Andrew Mackenzie and the whole team at Channel 4 for their total support and vision through all three series.

I'd of course like to thank everyone at Dragonfly, including Sanjay Singhal and Sarah Faulds. And I'm particularly indebted to Nick Curwin and Magnus Temple – thank you, gents.

I'd also like to acknowledge the toil and talent of the superb cameramen I've been lucky enough to work with over the last couple of years – in particular the fabulous Jan Pester, Don Freeman, Brendan Easton and, of course, Will Milner. They are brilliant at what they do, and they are proper mens' men. Other people on the TV side that must be gratefully thanked for their combination of good humour, total professionalism and hard work are: Justine Tyler, Abigail Watts, Josephine Grant, Katy Southwood and Jenny Hargreaves.

And a special thank you to the man who was Charlie to all us angels – the one and only Richard Yee, the show's architect, and a man responsible for the consistent tone and occasional integrity of the series.

This book itself wouldn't have happened without a small number of scrumptious human beings. First and foremost, my amazing editor Natalie Jerome, who took a chance on me and kept the faith throughout: thank you, Natalie. My literary agent Gordon Wise, who did a brilliant job across the board and put up with my occasional periods of radio silence ... Wayne Davison at Shine whose guile and positive energy throughout was key to making it happen. And finally my agent Janette Linden, Patrick Bustin and the whole team at PBJ, who are simply fantastic.

Acknowledgements

For their love I'd like to thank Shay, Lorraine and Yvonne. And my parents, Seamus and Diane, who gave me everything, and which I will never be able to repay.

To my boys for the joy they bring every day.

And finally to my wife and best friend Maria Rosa – thank you for literally everything – I love you.

'Extra' Extraordinary!

For more information about Mark and his amazing journeys, log on to WWW.MARKDOLAN.COM for exclusive video footage, photos and features.

You can also find out about Mark's nationwide search for Britain's most extraordinary person.

And log on to the above address to download an audio bonus chapter.